MANHATTAN GMAT

Geometry

GMAT Strategy Guide

This comprehensive guide illustrates every geometric principle, formula, and problem type tested on the GMAT. Understand and master the intricacies of shapes, planes, lines, angles, and objects.

guide **4**

Geometry GMAT Strategy Guide, Fifth Edition

10-digit International Standard Book Number: 1-935707-64-7
13-digit International Standard Book Number: 978-1-935707-64-6
eISBN: 978-1-937707-05-7

Note: *GMAT, Graduate Management Admission Test, Graduate Management Admission
Council,* and *GMAC* are all registered trademarks of the Graduate Management Admission
Council, which neither sponsors nor is affiliated in any way with this product.

Layout Design: Dan McNaney and Cathy Huang
Cover Design: Evyn Williams and Dan McNaney
Cover Photography: Alli Ugosoli

INSTRUCTIONAL GUIDE SERIES

SUPPLEMENTAL GUIDE SERIES

MANHATTAN
GMAT

April 24th, 2012

Dear Student,

Thank you for picking up a copy of *Geometry*. I hope this book provides just the guidance you need to get the most out of your GMAT studies.

As with most accomplishments, there were many people involved in the creation of the book you are holding. First and foremost is Zeke Vanderhoek, the founder of Manhattan GMAT. Zeke was a lone tutor in New York when he started the company in 2000. Now, 12 years later, the company has instructors and offices nationwide and contributes to the studies and successes of thousands of students each year.

Our Manhattan GMAT Strategy Guides are based on the continuing experiences of our instructors and students. For this volume, we are particularly indebted to Stacey Koprince and Dave Mahler. Dave deserves special recognition for his contributions over the past number of years. Dan McNaney and Cathy Huang provided their design expertise to make the books as user-friendly as possible, and Noah Teitelbaum and Liz Krisher made sure all the moving pieces came together at just the right time. And there's Chris Ryan. Beyond providing additions and edits for this book, Chris continues to be the driving force behind all of our curriculum efforts. His leadership is invaluable. Finally, thank you to all of the Manhattan GMAT students who have provided input and feedback over the years. This book wouldn't be half of what it is without your voice.

At Manhattan GMAT, we continually aspire to provide the best instructors and resources possible. We hope that you'll find our commitment manifest in this book. If you have any questions or comments, please email me at dgonzalez@manhattangmat.com. I'll look forward to reading your comments, and I'll be sure to pass them along to our curriculum team.

Thanks again, and best of luck preparing for the GMAT!

Sincerely,

Dan

Dan Gonzalez
President
Manhattan GMAT

HOW TO ACCESS YOUR ONLINE RESOURCES

If you…

➤ ### are a registered Manhattan GMAT student

and have received this book as part of your course materials, you have AUTOMATIC access to ALL of our online resources. This includes all practice exams, question banks, and online updates to this book. To access these resources, follow the instructions in the Welcome Guide provided to you at the start of your program. Do NOT follow the instructions below.

➤ ### purchased this book from the Manhattan GMAT online store or at one of our centers

1. Go to: www.manhattanprep.com/gmat/studentcenter.

2. Log in using the username and password used when your account was set up.

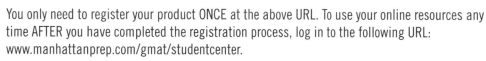

➤ ### purchased this book at a retail location

1. Create an account with Manhattan GMAT at the website: www.manhattanprep.com/gmat/register.

2. Go to: www.manhattanprep.com/gmat/access.

3. Follow the instructions on the screen.

Your one year of online access begins on the day that you register your book at the above URL.

You only need to register your product ONCE at the above URL. To use your online resources any time AFTER you have completed the registration process, log in to the following URL: www.manhattanprep.com/gmat/studentcenter.

Please note that online access is nontransferable. This means that only NEW and UNREGISTERED copies of the book will grant you online access. Previously used books will NOT provide any online resources.

➤ ### purchased an eBook version of this book

1. Create an account with Manhattan GMAT at the website: www.manhattanprep.com/gmat/register.

2. Email a copy of your purchase receipt to gmat@manhattanprep.com to activate your resources. Please be sure to use the same email address to create an account that you used to purchase the eBook.

For any technical issues, email techsupport@manhattanprep.com or call 800-576-4628.

Please refer to the following page for a description of the online resources that come with this book.

YOUR ONLINE RESOURCES

Your purchase includes ONLINE ACCESS to the following:

⊛ 6 Computer-Adaptive Online Practice Exams

The 6 full-length computer-adaptive practice exams included with the purchase of this book are delivered online using Manhattan GMAT's proprietary computer-adaptive test engine. The exams adapt to your ability level by drawing from a bank of more than 1,200 unique questions of varying difficulty levels written by Manhattan GMAT's expert instructors, all of whom have scored in the 99th percentile on the Official GMAT. At the end of each exam you will receive a score, an analysis of your results, and the opportunity to review detailed explanations for each question. You may choose to take the exams timed or untimed.

The content presented in this book is updated periodically to ensure that it reflects the GMAT's most current trends and is as accurate as possible. You may view any known errors or minor changes upon registering for online access.

Important Note: The 6 computer adaptive online exams included with the purchase of this book are the SAME exams that you receive upon purchasing ANY book in the Manhattan GMAT Complete Strategy Guide Set.

⊛ *Geometry* Online Question Bank

The Bonus Online Question Bank for *Geometry* consists of 25 extra practice questions (with detailed explanations) that test the variety of concepts and skills covered in this book. These questions provide you with extra practice beyond the problem sets contained in this book. You may use our online timer to practice your pacing by setting time limits for each question in the bank.

⊛ Online Updates to the Contents in this Book

The content presented in this book is updated periodically to ensure that it reflects the GMAT's most current trends. You may view all updates, including any known errors or changes, upon registering for online access.

TABLE *of* CONTENTS

guide **4**

Chapter 1 *of* Geometry

Polygons

In This Chapter...

Chapter 1:

Polygons

A polygon is defined as a closed shape formed by line segments. The polygons tested on the GMAT include the following:

- Three-sided shapes (Triangles)
- Four-sided shapes (Quadrilaterals)
- Other polygons with *n* sides (where *n* is five or more)

This section will focus on polygons of four or more sides. In particular, the GMAT emphasizes quadrilaterals — or four-sided polygons — including trapezoids, parallelograms, and special parallelograms, such as rhombuses, rectangles, and squares.

Polygons are two-dimensional shapes — they lie in a plane. The GMAT tests your ability to work with different measurements associated with polygons. The measurements you must be adept with are (1) interior angles, (2) perimeter, and (3) area.

The GMAT also tests your knowledge of three-dimensional shapes formed from polygons, particularly rectangular solids and cubes. The measurements you must be adept with are (1) surface area and (2) volume.

Quadrilaterals: An Overview

The most common polygon tested on the GMAT, aside from the triangle, is the quadrilateral (any four-sided polygon). Almost all GMAT polygon problems involve the special types of quadrilaterals shown below.

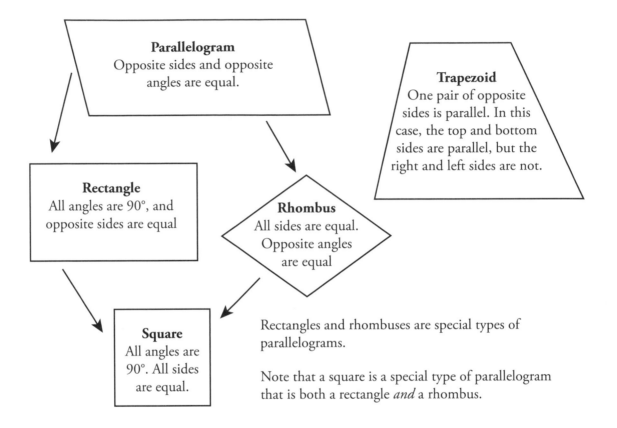

Rectangles and rhombuses are special types of parallelograms.

Note that a square is a special type of parallelogram that is both a rectangle *and* a rhombus.

Polygons and Interior Angles

The sum of the interior angles of a given polygon depends only on the **number of sides in the polygon**. The following chart displays the relationship between the type of polygon and the sum of its interior angles.

The sum of the interior angles of a polygon follows a specific pattern that depends on n, the number of sides that the polygon has. This sum is always 180° times 2 less than n (the number of sides).

Polygon	# of Sides	Sum of Interior Angles
Triangle	3	180°
Quadrilateral	4	360°
Pentagon	5	540°
Hexagon	6	720°

1

This pattern can be expressed with the following formula:

$$(n - 2) \times 180 = \text{Sum of Interior Angles of a Polygon}$$

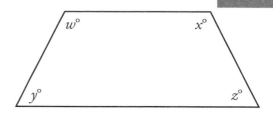

Since this polygon has four sides, the sum of its interior angles is $(4 - 2)180 = 2(180) = 360°$.

Alternatively, note that a quadrilateral can be cut into two triangles by a line connecting opposite corners. Thus, the sum of the angles = $2(180) = 360°$.

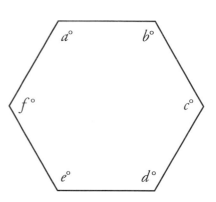

Since the next polygon has six sides, the sum of its interior angles is $(6 - 2)180 = 4(180) = 720°$.

Alternatively, note that a hexagon can be cut into four triangles by three lines connecting corners.

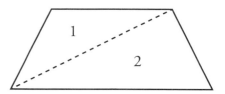

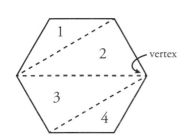

Thus, the sum of the angles = $4(180) = 720°$.

By the way, the corners of polygons are also known as vertices (singular: vertex).

Polygons and Perimeter

The perimeter refers to the distance around a polygon, or the sum of the lengths of all the sides. The amount of fencing needed to surround a yard would be equivalent to the perimeter of that yard (the sum of all the sides).

The perimeter of the pentagon to the right is:
    $9 + 7 + 4 + 6 + 5 = 31$.

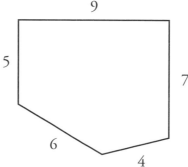

1

Polygons and Area

The area of a polygon refers to the space inside the polygon. Area is measured in square units, such as cm² (square centimeters), m² (square meters), or ft² (square feet). For example, the amount of space that a garden occupies is the area of that garden.

On the GMAT, there are two polygon area formulas you *must* know:

1) Area of a TRIANGLE = $\dfrac{\text{Base} \times \text{Height}}{2}$

The base refers to the bottom side of the triangle. The height *always* refers to a line drawn from the opposite vertex to the base, creating a 90° angle.

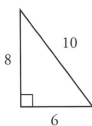

In this triangle, the base is 6 and the height (perpendicular to the base) is 8. The area = (6 × 8) ÷ 2 = 48 ÷ 2 = 24.

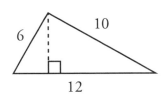

In this triangle, the base is 12, but the height is not shown. Neither of the other two sides of the triangle is perpendicular to the base. In order to find the area of this triangle, you would first need to determine the height, which is represented by the dotted line.

2) Area of a RECTANGLE = **Length × Width**

The length of this rectangle is 13, and the width is 4. Therefore, the area = 13 × 4 = 52.

The GMAT will occasionally ask you to find the area of a polygon more complex than a simple triangle or rectangle. The following formulas can be used to find the areas of other types of quadrilaterals:

3) Area of a TRAPEZOID = $\dfrac{(\text{Base}_1 + \text{Base}_2) \times \text{Height}}{2}$

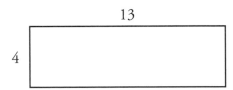

Note that the height refers to a line perpendicular to the two bases, which are parallel. (You often have to draw in the height, as in this case.) In the trapezoid shown, base$_1$ = 18, base$_2$ = 6, and the height = 8. The area = (18 + 6) × 8 ÷ 2 = 96. Another way to think about this is to take the *average* of the two bases and multiply it by the height.

MANHATTAN
GMAT

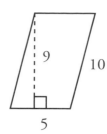

4) Area of any PARALLELOGRAM = **Base** × **Height**

Note that the height refers to the line perpendicular to the base. (As with the trapezoid, you often have to draw in the height.) In the parallelogram shown, the base = 5 and the height = 9. Therefore, the area is 5 × 9 = 45.

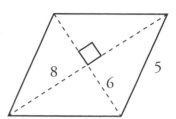

5) Area of a RHOMBUS = $\dfrac{\textbf{Diagonal}_1 \times \textbf{Diagonal}_2}{\textbf{2}}$

Note that the diagonals of a rhombus are *always* perpendicular bisectors (meaning that they cut each other in half at a 90° angle).

The area of this rhombus is $\dfrac{6 \times 8}{2} = \dfrac{48}{2} = 24$.

Although these formulas are very useful to memorize for the GMAT, you may notice that all of the above shapes can actually be divided into some combination of rectangles and right triangles. Therefore, if you forget the area formula for a particular shape, simply cut the shape into rectangles and right triangles, and then find the areas of these individual pieces. For example:

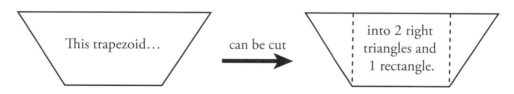

3 Dimensions: Surface Area

The GMAT tests two particular three-dimensional shapes formed from polygons: the rectangular solid and the cube. Note that a cube is just a special type of rectangular solid.

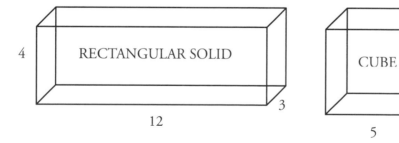

The surface area of a three-dimensional shape is the amount of space on the surface of that particular object. For example, the amount of paint that it would take to fully cover a rectangular box could be determined by finding the surface area of that box. As with simple area, surface area is measured in square units such as inches^2 (square inches) or ft^2 (square feet).

1

Surface Area = the *sum* of *all* of the faces

Both a rectangular solid and a cube have **six faces**.

To determine the surface area of a rectangular solid, you must find the area of each face. Notice, however, that in a rectangular solid, the front and back faces have the same area, the top and bottom faces have the same area, and the two side faces have the same area. In the solid on the previous page, the area of the front face is equal to $12 \times 4 = 48$. Thus, the back face also has an area of 48. The area of the bottom face is equal to $12 \times 3 = 36$. Thus, the top face also has an area of 36. Finally, each side face has an area of $3 \times 4 = 12$. Therefore, the surface area, or the sum of the areas of all six faces equals $48(2) + 36(2) + 12(2) = 192$.

To determine the surface area of a cube, you only need the length of one side. You can see from the cube on the previous page that a cube is made of six square surfaces. First, find the area of one face: $5 \times 5 = 25$. Then, multiply by six to account for all of the faces: $6 \times 25 = 150$.

3 Dimensions: Volume

The volume of a three-dimensional shape is the amount of "stuff" it can hold. "Capacity" is another word for volume. For example, the amount of liquid that a rectangular milk carton holds can be determined by finding the volume of the carton. Volume is measured in cubic units such as inches^3 (cubic inches), ft^3 (cubic feet), or m^3 (cubic meters).

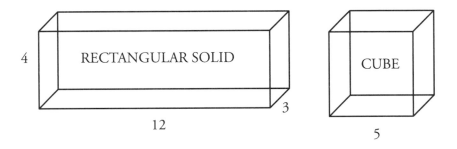

Volume = Length × Width × Height

By looking at the rectangular solid above, you can see that the length is 12, the width is 3, and the height is 4. Therefore, the volume is $12 \times 3 \times 4 = 144$.

In a cube, all three of the dimensions—length, width, and height—are identical. Therefore, knowing the measurement of just one side of the cube is sufficient to find the volume. In the cube above, the volume is $5 \times 5 \times 5 = 125$.

1

Beware of a GMAT volume trick:

> How many books, each with a volume of 100 in^3, can be packed into a crate with a volume of 5,000 in^3?

It is tempting to answer "50 books" (since $50 \times 100 = 5,000$). However, this is incorrect, because you do not know the exact dimensions of each book! One book might be $5 \times 5 \times 4$, while another book might be $20 \times 5 \times 1$. Even though both have a volume of 100 in^3, they have different rectangular shapes. Without knowing the exact shapes of all the books, you cannot tell whether they would all fit into the crate. Remember, when you are fitting 3-dimensional objects into other 3-dimensional objects, knowing the respective volumes is not enough. You must know the specific dimensions (length, width, and height) of each object to determine whether the objects can fit without leaving gaps.

Problem Set (Note: Figures are not drawn to scale.)

1. Frank the Fencemaker needs to fence in a rectangular yard. He fences in the entire yard, except for one full side of the yard, which equals 40 feet. The yard has an area of 280 square feet. How many feet of fence does Frank use?

2. A pentagon has three sides with length x, and two sides with the length $3x$. If x is $\frac{2}{3}$ of an inch, what is the perimeter of the pentagon?

3. $ABCD$ is a quadrilateral, with AB parallel to CD (see figure). E is a point between C and D such that AE represents the height of $ABCD$, and E is the midpoint of CD. If AB is 4 inches long, AE is 5 inches long, and the area of triangle AED is 12.5 square inches, what is the area of $ABCD$? (Note: figure not drawn to scale.)

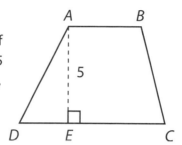

4. A rectangular tank needs to be coated with insulation. The tank has dimensions of 4 feet, 5 feet, and 2.5 feet. Each square foot of insulation costs $20. How much will it cost to cover the surface of the tank with insulation?

5. 40 percent of Andrea's living room floor is covered by a carpet that is 4 feet by 9 feet. What is the area of her living room floor?

6. If the perimeter of a rectangular flower bed is 30 feet, and its area is 44 square feet, what is the length of each of its shorter sides?

7. There is a rectangular parking lot with a length of $2x$ and a width of x. What is the ratio of the perimeter of the parking lot to the area of the parking lot, in terms of x?

8. A rectangular solid has a square base, with each side of the base measuring 4 meters. If the volume of the solid is 112 cubic meters, what is the surface area of the solid?

9. A swimming pool has a length of 30 meters, a width of 10 meters, and an average depth of 2 meters. If a hose can fill the pool at a rate of 0.5 cubic meters per minute, how many hours will it take the hose to fill the pool?

P

10. *ABCD* is a square picture frame (see figure). *EFGH* is a square inscribed within *ABCD* as a space for a picture. The area of *EFGH* (for the picture) is equal to the area of the picture frame (the area of *ABCD* minus the area of *EFGH*). If *AB* = 6, what is the length of *EF*?

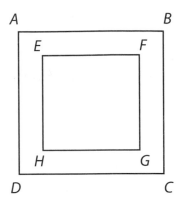

Solutions

P

1. **54 feet:** You know that one side of the yard is 40 feet long; call this the length. You also know that the area of the yard is 280 square feet. In order to determine the perimeter, you must know the width of the yard.

$$A = l \times w$$
$$280 = 40w$$
$$w = 280 \div 40 = 7 \text{ feet}$$

Frank fences in the two 7-foot sides and one of the 40-foot sides. $40 + 2(7) = 54$.

2. **6 inches:** The perimeter of a pentagon is the sum of its five sides: $x + x + x + 3x + 3x = 9x$. If x is 2/3 of an inch, the perimeter is $9(2/3)$, or 6 inches.

3. **35 in²:** If E is the midpoint of C, then $CE = DE = x$. You can determine the length of x by using what you know about the area of triangle AED:

$$A = \frac{b \times h}{2}$$
$$12.5 = \frac{5x}{2}$$
$$25 = 5x$$ Therefore, the length of CD is $2x$, or 10.
$$x = 5$$

To find the area of the trapezoid, use the formula:

$$A = \frac{b_1 + b_2}{2} \times h$$
$$= \frac{4 + 10}{2} \times 5$$
$$= 35 \text{ in}^2$$

4. **$1,700:** To find the surface area of a rectangular solid, sum the individual areas of all six faces:

	Area of one face		Total area of two identical faces
Top and Bottom:	$5 \times 4 = 20$	→	$20 \times 2 = 40$
Side 1:	$5 \times 2.5 = 12.5$	→	$12.5 \times 2 = 25$
Side 2:	$4 \times 2.5 = 10$	→	$10 \times 2 = 20$
All 6 faces	→		$40 + 25 + 20 = 85 \text{ ft}^2$

Covering the entire tank will cost $85 \times \$20 = \$1,700$.

P

5. 90 ft²: The area of the carpet is equal to $l \times w$, or 36 ft². Set up a proportion to find the area of the whole living room floor:

$$\frac{40}{100} = \frac{36}{x}$$

Cross-multiply to solve.

$$40x = 3,600$$
$$x = 90 \text{ ft}^2$$

6. 4: Set up equations to represent the area and perimeter of the flower bed:

$$A = l \times w \qquad\qquad P = 2(l + w)$$

Then, substitute the known values for the variables A and P:

$$44 = l \times w \qquad\qquad 30 = 2(l + w)$$

Solve the two equations with the substitution method:

$$l = \frac{44}{w}$$

$$30 = 2\left(\frac{44}{w} + w\right)$$

Multiply the entire equation by $\frac{w}{2}$.

$$15w = 44 + w^2$$

Solving the quadratic equation yields two solutions: 4 and 11. Each represents a possible side length. Since you were asked to find the length of the shorter side, the answer is the smaller of the two possible values, 4.

$$w^2 - 15w + 44 = 0$$
$$(w - 11)(w - 4) = 0$$
$$w = \{4, 11\}$$

Alternatively, you can arrive at the correct solution by picking numbers. What length and width add up to 15 (half of the perimeter) and multiply to produce 44 (the area)? Some experimentation will demonstrate that the longer side must be 11 and the shorter side must be 4.

7. $\frac{3}{x}$ or 3:x: If the length of the parking lot is $2x$ and the width is x, you can set up a fraction to represent the ratio of the perimeter to the area as follows:

$$\frac{\text{perimeter}}{\text{area}} = \frac{2(2x + x)}{(2x)(x)} = \frac{6x}{2x^2} = \frac{3}{x}$$

8. 144 m²: The volume of a rectangular solid equals (length) × (width) × (height). If you know that the length and width are both 4 meters long, you can substitute values into the formulas as shown:

$$112 = 4 \times 4 \times h$$
$$h = 7$$

P

To find the surface area of a rectangular solid, sum the individual areas of all six faces:

	Area of one face		Total area of two identical faces
Top and Bottom:	$4 \times 4 = 16$	→	$2 \times 16 = 32$
Sides:	$4 \times 7 = 28$	→	$4 \times 28 = 112$
All 6 faces	→		$32 + 112 = 144 \text{ m}^2$

9. **20 hours:** The volume of the pool is (length) × (width) × (height), or $30 \times 10 \times 2 = 600$ cubic meters. Use a standard work equation, $RT = W$, where W represents the total work of 600 m³:

$$0.5t = 600$$
$$t = 1{,}200 \text{ minutes}$$

Convert this time to hours by dividing by 60: $1{,}200 \div 60 = 20$ hours.

Alternately, we could convert first: 0.5 m³/min × 60 min/hr = 30 m³/hr. Next, use the standard work equation:

$$30t = 600$$
$$t = 20 \text{ hours.}$$

10. $3\sqrt{2}$: The area of the frame and the area of the picture sum to the total area of the image, which is 6^2, or 36. Therefore, the area of the frame and the picture are each equal to half of 36, or 18. Since *EFGH* is a square, the length of *EF* is $\sqrt{18}$, or $3\sqrt{2}$.

Chapter 2
of Geometry

Triangles & Diagonals

In This Chapter...

Chapter 2:
Triangles & Diagonals

The polygon most commonly tested on the GMAT is the triangle.

Right triangles (those with a 90° angle) require particular attention, because they have special properties that are useful for solving many GMAT geometry problems.

The most important property of a right triangle is the unique relationship of the three sides. Given the lengths of any two of the sides of a right triangle, you can determine the length of the third side using the Pythagorean Theorem. There are even two special types of right triangles—the 30–60–90 triangle and the 45–45–90 triangle—for which you only need the length of *one* side to determine the lengths of the other two sides.

Finally, right triangles are essential for solving problems involving other polygons. For instance, you might cut more complex polygons into right triangles.

The Angles of a Triangle

The angles in any given triangle have two key properties:

(1) **The sum of the three angles of a triangle equals 180°.**

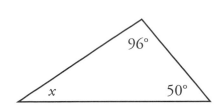

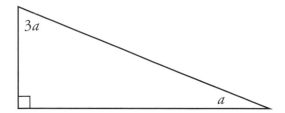

What is *x*? Since the sum of the three angles must be 180°, you can solve for *x* as follows:
$180 - 96 - 50 = x = 34°.$

What is *a*? Since the sum of the three angles must be 180°, you can solve for *x* as follows:

$90 + 3a + a = 180 \longrightarrow a = 22.5°.$

2

(2) **Angles correspond to their opposite sides.** This means that the largest angle is opposite the longest side, while the smallest angle is opposite the shortest side. Additionally, **if two sides are equal, their opposite angles are also equal.** Such triangles are called **isosceles** triangles.

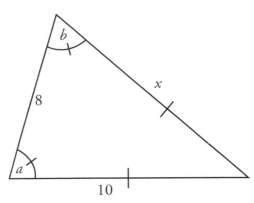

If angle a = angle b, what is the length of side x?

Since the side opposite angle b has a length of 10, the side opposite angle a must have the same length. Therefore, $x = 10$.

Mark equal angles and equal sides with a slash, as shown. Also be ready to redraw; often, a triangle that you know is isosceles is not displayed as such. To help your intuition, redraw the triangle to scale.

The Sides of a Triangle

Consider the following "impossible" triangle $\triangle ABC$ and what it reveals about the relationship between the three sides of any triangle.

The triangle to the right could never be drawn with the given measurements. Why? Consider that the short-est distance between any two points is a straight line. According to the triangle shown, the direct straight line distance between point C and point B is 14; however, the indirect path from point C to B (the path that goes from C to A to B) is 10 + 3, or 13, which is shorter than the direct path! This is clearly impossible.

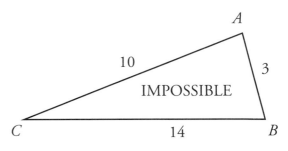

The above example leads to the following Triangle Inequality Law:

The sum of any two sides of a triangle must be *greater than* the third side.

Therefore, the maximum integer distance for side BC in the triangle above is 12. If the length of side BC is not restricted to integers, then this length has to be **less than** 13.

Note that the length cannot be as small as we wish, either. It must be **greater than** the difference be-tween the lengths of the other two sides. In this case, side BC must be longer than 10 − 3 = 7. This is a consequence of the same idea.

Consider the following triangle and the proof that the given measurements are possible:

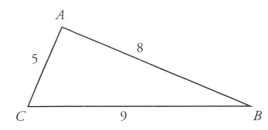

Test each combination of sides to prove that the measurements of this triangle are possible.

$5 + 8 > 9$
$5 + 9 > 8$
$8 + 9 > 5$

2

Note that the sum of two sides cannot be equal to the third side. The sum of two sides must always be **greater than** the third side.

If you are given two sides of a triangle, the length of the third side must lie between the difference and the sum of the two given sides. For instance, if you are told that two sides are of length 3 and 4, then the length of the third side must be between 1 and 7.

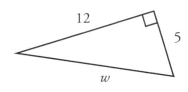

The Pythagorean Theorem

A right triangle is a triangle with one right angle (90°). Every right triangle is composed of two **legs** and a **hypotenuse**. The hypotenuse is the side opposite the right angle and is often assigned the letter c. The two legs which form the right angle are often called a and b (it does not matter which leg is a and which leg is b).

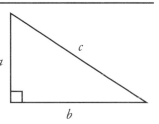

Given the lengths of two sides of a right triangle, how can you determine the length of the third side? Use the Pythagorean Theorem, which states that the sum of the square of the two legs of a right triangle ($a^2 + b^2$) is equal to the square of the hypotenuse of that triangle (c^2).

Pythagorean Theorem: $a^2 + b^2 = c^2$

What is x?

$a^2 + b^2 = c^2$
$x^2 + 6^2 = 10^2$
$x^2 + 36 = 100$
$x^2 = 64$
$x = 8$

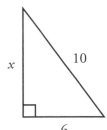

What is w?

$a^2 + b^2 = c^2$
$5^2 + 12^2 = w^2$
$25 + 144 = w^2$
$169 = w^2$
$13 = w$

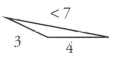

Common Right Triangles

Certain right triangles appear over and over on the GMAT. It pays to memorize these common combinations in order to save time on the exam. Instead of using the Pythagorean Theorem to solve for the lengths of the sides of these common right triangles, you should know the following Pythagorean triples from memory:

Common Combinations	Key Multiples
3–4–5 The most popular of all right triangles $3^2 + 4^2 = 5^2$ ($9 + 16 = 25$)	6–8–10 9–12–15 12–16–20
5–12–13 Also quite popular on the GMAT $5^2 + 12^2 = 13^2$ ($25 + 144 = 169$)	10–24–26
8–15–17 This one appears less frequently $8^2 + 15^2 = 17^2$ ($64 + 225 = 289$)	None

Watch out for impostor triangles! A non-right triangle with one side equal to 3 and another side equal to 4 does not *necessarily* have a third side of length 5.

Isosceles Triangles and the 45–45–90 Triangle

As previously noted, an isosceles triangle is one in which two sides are equal. The two angles opposite those two sides will also be equal. The most important isosceles triangle on the GMAT is the isosceles right triangle.

An isosceles right triangle has one 90° angle (opposite the hypotenuse) and two 45° angles (opposite the two equal legs). This triangle is called the 45–45–90 triangle.

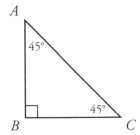

The lengths of the legs of every 45–45–90 triangle have a specific ratio, which you must memorize:

45° ➞ 45° ➞ 90°		
leg	leg	hypotenuse
1 :	**1** :	$\sqrt{2}$
x :	x :	$x\sqrt{2}$

MANHATTAN
GMAT

Given that the length of side *AB* is 5, what are the lengths of sides *BC* and *AC*?

Since *AB* is 5, use the ratio $1:1:\sqrt{2}$ for sides $AB:BC:AC$ to determine that the multiplier *x* is 5. You then find that the sides of the triangle have lengths $5:5:5\sqrt{2}$. Therefore, the length of side *BC* = 5, and the length of side $AC = 5\sqrt{2}$.

Given that the length of side *AC* is $\sqrt{18}$, what are the lengths of sides *AB* and *BC*?

Since the hypotenuse *AC* is $\sqrt{18} = x\sqrt{2}$, you find that $x = \sqrt{18} \div \sqrt{2} = \sqrt{9} = 3$. Thus, the sides *AB* and *BC* are each equal to *x*, or 3.

One reason that the 45–45–90 triangle is so important is that this triangle is exactly half of a square! That is, two 45–45–90 triangles put together make up a square. Thus, if you are given the diagonal of a square, you can use the 45–45–90 ratio to find the length of a side of the square.

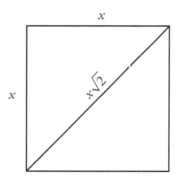

Equilateral Triangles and the 30–60–90 Triangle

An equilateral triangle is one in which all three sides (and all three angles) are equal. Each angle of an equilateral triangle is 60° (because all 3 angles must sum to 180°). A close relative of the equilateral triangle is the 30–60–90 triangle. Notice that two of these triangles, when put together, form an equilateral triangle:

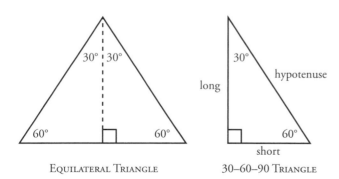

EQUILATERAL TRIANGLE   30–60–90 TRIANGLE

The lengths of the legs of every 30–60–90 triangle have the following ratio, which you must memorize:

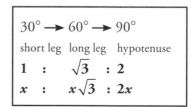

2

Given that the short leg of a 30–60–90 triangle has a length of 6, what are the lengths of the long leg and the hypotenuse?

The short leg, which is opposite the 30 degree angle, is 6. Use the ratio $1 : \sqrt{3} : 2$ to determine that the multiplier x is 6. You then find that the sides of the triangle have lengths $6 : 6\sqrt{3} : 12$. The long leg measures $6\sqrt{3}$ and the hypotenuse measures 12.

Given that an equilateral triangle has a side of length 10, what is its height?

Looking at the equilateral triangle above, you can see that the side of an equilateral triangle is the same as the hypotenuse of a 30–60–90 triangle. Additionally, the height of an equilateral triangle is the same as the long leg of a 30–60–90 triangle. Since you are told that the hypotenuse is 10, use the ratio $x : x\sqrt{3} : 2x$ to set $2x = 10$ and determine that the multiplier x is 5. You then find that the sides of the 30–60–90 triangle have lengths $5 : 5\sqrt{3} : 10$. Thus, the long leg has a length of $5\sqrt{3}$, which is the height of the equilateral triangle.

If you get tangled up on a 30–60–90 triangle, try to find the length of the short leg. The other legs will then be easier to figure out.

Diagonals of Other Polygons

Right triangles are useful for more than just triangle problems. They are also helpful for finding the diagonals of other polygons, specifically squares, cubes, rectangles, and rectangular solids.

The diagonal of a square can be found using this formula:

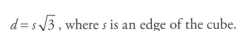

   $d = s\sqrt{2}$, where s is a side of the square.
   This is also the face diagonal of a cube.

The main diagonal of a cube can be found using this formula:

   $d = s\sqrt{3}$, where s is an edge of the cube.

Given a square with a side of length 5, what is the length of the diagonal of the square?

Using the formula $d = s\sqrt{2}$, you find that the length of the diagonal of the square is $5\sqrt{2}$.

What is the measure of an edge of a cube with a main diagonal of length $\sqrt{60}$?

Again, using the formula $d = s\sqrt{3}$, solve as follows:

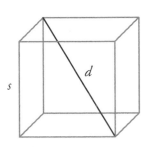

$$\sqrt{60} = s\sqrt{3} \rightarrow s = \frac{\sqrt{60}}{\sqrt{3}} = \sqrt{20}$$

2

Thus, the length of the edge of the cube is $\sqrt{20}$.

To find the diagonal of a rectangle, you must know *either* the length and the width *or* one dimension and the proportion of one to the other.

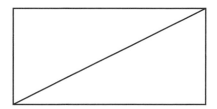

If the rectangle to the left has a length of 12 and a width of 5, what is the length of the diagonal?

Using the Pythagorean Theorem, solve:
$5^2 + 12^2 = c^2 \rightarrow 25 + 144 = c^2 \rightarrow c = 13$

The diagonal length is 13. Alternatively, note that this is a right triangle and you know two of the sides are 5 and 12. This is a common right triangle, so you know the length of the hypotenuse is 13.

If the rectangle above has a width of 6, and the ratio of the width to the length is 3:4, what is the diagonal?

Using the ratio, you find that the length is 8. Then you can use the Pythagorean Theorem. Alternatively, you can recognize that this is a 6–8–10 triangle. Either way, you find that the diagonal length is 10.

What is the length of the main diagonal of this rectangular solid?

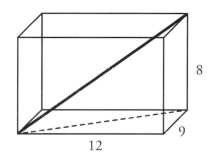

To find the diagonal of a rectangular solid, you can use the Pythagorean Theorem twice.

First, find the diagonal of the bottom face: $9^2 + 12^2 = c^2$ yields $c = 15$ (this is a multiple of a 3–4–5 triangle), so the bottom (dashed) diagonal is 15. Then, you can consider this bottom diagonal of length 15 as the base leg of another right triangle with a height of 8. Now use the Pythagorean Theorem a second time: $8^2 + 15^2 = c^2$ yields $c = 17$, so the main diagonal is 17.

Generalizing this approach, you find the "Deluxe" Pythagorean Theorem: $d^2 = x^2 + y^2 + z^2$, where x, y, and z are the sides of the rectangular solid and d is the main diagonal. In this case, you could also solve this problem by applying the equation $9^2 + 12^2 + 8^2 = d^2$, yielding $d = 17$.

Similar Triangles

One final tool that you can use for GMAT triangle problems is the similar triangle strategy. Often, looking for similar triangles can help you solve complex problems.

Triangles are defined as similar if all their corresponding angles are **equal** and their **corresponding sides are in proportion**.

 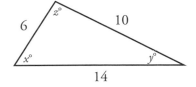

Once you find that 2 triangles have 2 pairs of equal angles, you know that the triangles are similar. If 2 sets of angles are congruent, then the third set of angles must be congruent, since the sum of the angles in any triangle is 180°.

What is the length of side *EF*?

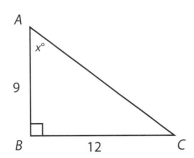 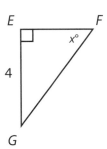

You know that the two triangles above are similar, because they have 2 angles in common (*x* and the right angle). Since they are similar triangles, their corresponding sides must be in proportion.

Side *BC* corresponds to side *EG* (since they both are opposite angle *x*). Since these sides are in the ratio of 12 : 4, you can determine that the large triangle is three times bigger than the smaller one. That is, the triangles are in the ratio of 3 : 1. Since side *AB* corresponds to side *EF*, and *AB* has a length of 9, you can conclude that side *EF* has a length of 3.

If you go on to compute the areas of these two triangles, you get the following results:

$$\text{Area of } ABC = \frac{1}{2}bh \qquad\qquad \text{Area of } EFG = \frac{1}{2}bh$$
$$= \frac{1}{2}(9)(12) \qquad\qquad\quad = \frac{1}{2}(3)(4)$$
$$= 54 \qquad\qquad\qquad\quad = 6$$

MANHATTAN
GMAT

These two areas are in the ratio of $54:6$, or $9:1$. Notice the connection between this $9:1$ ratio of areas and the $3:1$ ratio of side lengths. The $9:1$ ratio is simply the $3:1$ ratio *squared*.

This observation can be generalized:

> **If two similar triangles have corresponding side lengths in ratio $a:b$, then their areas will be in ratio $a^2:b^2$.**

The lengths being compared do not have to be sides—they can represent heights or perimeters. In fact, the figures do not have to be triangles. The principle holds true for *any* similar figures: quadrilaterals, pentagons, etc. For similar solids with corresponding sides in ratio $a:b$, their volumes will be in ratio $a^3:b^3$.

Triangles and Area, Revisited

Although you may commonly think of "the base" of a triangle as whichever side is drawn horizontally, you can designate any side of a triangle as the base. For example, the following three diagrams show the same triangle, with each side in turn designated as the base:

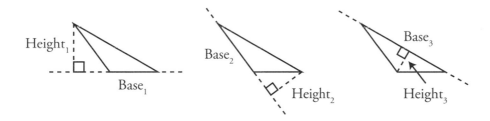

Since a triangle only has one area, the area must be the same regardless of the side chosen as the base. In other words,

$$\frac{1}{2} \times \text{Base}_1 \times \text{Height}_1 = \frac{1}{2} \times \text{Base}_2 \times \text{Height}_2 = \frac{1}{2} \times \text{Base}_3 \times \text{Height}_3$$

and therefore

$$\text{Base}_1 \times \text{Height}_1 = \text{Base}_2 \times \text{Height}_2 = \text{Base}_3 \times \text{Height}_3$$

Right triangles have three possible bases just as other triangles do, but they are special because their two legs are perpendicular. Therefore, if one of the legs is chosen as the base, then the other leg is the height. Of course, you can also choose the hypotenuse as the base.

2

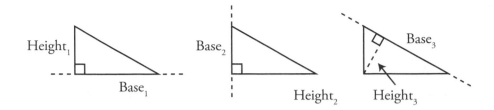

Thus, the area of a right triangle is given by the following formulas:

$$A = \frac{1}{2} \times \text{(One leg)} \times \text{(Other leg)} = \frac{1}{2} \text{ Hypotenuse} \times \text{Height from hypotenuse}$$

Because an **equilateral triangle** can be split into two 30–60–90 triangles, a useful formula can be derived for its area. If the side length of the equilateral triangle is S, then S is also the hypotenuse of each of the 30–60–90 triangles, so their sides are as shown in the diagram.

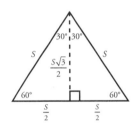

The equilateral triangle has base of length S and a height of length $\dfrac{S\sqrt{3}}{2}$.

Therefore, the **area of an equilateral triangle with a side of length S is**

equal to $\dfrac{1}{2}(S)\left(\dfrac{S\sqrt{3}}{2}\right) = \dfrac{S^2\sqrt{3}}{4}$.

Knowing this formula can save you significant time on a problem involving the area of an equilateral triangle, although you can always solve for the area without this formula.

Problem Set (Note: Figures are not drawn to scale.)

1. A square is bisected into two equal triangles (see figure). If the length of *BD* is $16\sqrt{2}$ inches, what is the area of the square?

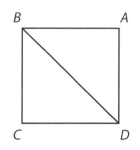

2. Beginning in Town A, Biker Bob rides his bike 10 miles west, 3 miles north, 5 miles east, and then 9 miles north, to Town B. How far apart are Town A and Town B? (Ignore the curvature of the earth.)

3. Triangle A has a base of *x* and a height of 2*x*. Triangle B is similar to Triangle A, and has a base of 2*x*. What is the ratio of the area of Triangle A to Triangle B?

4. What is the measure of angle *x* in the figure to the right?

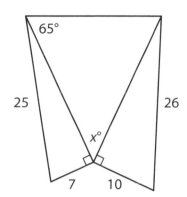

5. The size of a square computer screen is measured by the length of its diagonal. How much bigger is the visible area of a square 24-inch screen than the area of a square 20-inch screen?

6. In Triangle *ABC*, *AD* = *DB* = *DC* (see figure). Given that angle *DCB* is 60° and angle *ACD* is 20°, what is the measure of angle *x*?

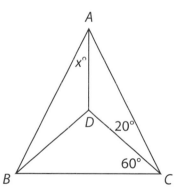

7. Two sides of a triangle are 4 and 10. If the third side is an integer *x*, how many possible values are there for *x*?

8. What is the area of an equilateral triangle whose sides measure 8 cm long?

9. Alexandra wants to pack away her posters without bending them. She rolls up the posters to put in a rectangular box that is 120 inches long, 90 inches wide, and 80 inches high. What is the longest a poster can be for Alexandra to pack it away without bending it (i.e., what is the diagonal of the rectangular box)?

10. The points of a six-pointed star consist of six identical equilateral triangles, with each side 4 cm (see figure). What is the area of the entire star, including the center?

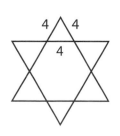

Solutions

1. **256 square units:** The diagonal of a square is $s\sqrt{2}$; therefore, the side length of square $ABCD$ is 16. The area of the square is s^2, or $16^2 = 256$.

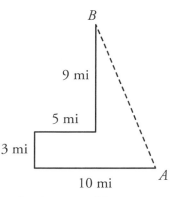

2. **13 miles:** If you draw a rough sketch of the path Biker Bob takes, as shown to the right, you can see that the direct distance from A to B forms the hypotenuse of a right triangle. The short leg (horizontal) is $10 - 5 = 5$ miles, and the long leg (vertical) is $9 + 3 = 12$ miles. Therefore, you can use the Pythagorean Theorem to find the direct distance from A to B:

$$5^2 + 12^2 = c^2$$
$$25 + 144 = c^2$$
$$c^2 = 169$$
$$c = 13$$

You might recognize the common right triangle: 5–12–13. If so, you don't need to use the Pythagorean theorem to calculate the value of 13.

3. **1 to 4:** Since you know that Triangle B is similar to Triangle A, you can set up a proportion to represent the relationship between the sides of both triangles:

$$\frac{\text{base}}{\text{height}} = \frac{x}{2x} = \frac{2x}{?}$$

By proportional reasoning, the height of Triangle B must be $4x$. Calculate the area of each triangle with the formula:

Triangle A: $A = \dfrac{b \times h}{2} = \dfrac{(x)(2x)}{2} = x^2$

Triangle B: $A = \dfrac{b \times h}{2} = \dfrac{(2x)(4x)}{2} = 4x^2$

The ratio of the area of Triangle A to Triangle B is 1 to 4. Alternatively, you can simply square the base ratio of 1 : 2.

4. **50°:** Use the Pythagorean Theorem to establish the missing lengths of the two right triangles on the right and left sides of the figure:

$$7^2 + b^2 = 25^2 \qquad\qquad 10^2 + b^2 = 26^2$$
$$49 + b^2 = 625 \qquad\qquad 100 + b^2 = 676$$
$$b^2 = 576 \qquad\qquad b^2 = 576$$
$$b = 24 \qquad\qquad b = 24$$

Alternatively, if you have the common right triangles memorized, notice that the second triangle (10–x–26) is the 5–12–13 triangle multiplied by 2. The missing length, therefore, is $12 \times 2 = 24$.

The inner triangle is isosceles. Therefore, both angles opposite the equal sides measure 65°. Since there are 180° in a right triangle, $x = 180 - 2(65) = 50°$.

P

5. **88 in²:** If the diagonal of the larger screen is 24 inches, and we know that $d = s\sqrt{2}$, then:

$$s = \frac{d}{\sqrt{2}} = \frac{24}{\sqrt{2}} = \frac{24(\sqrt{2})}{(\sqrt{2})(\sqrt{2})} = \frac{24\sqrt{2}}{2} = 12\sqrt{2}$$

By the same reasoning, the side length of the smaller screen is $\frac{20}{\sqrt{2}} = 10\sqrt{2}$.

The areas of the two screens are:

Large screen: $A = 12\sqrt{2} \times 12\sqrt{2} = 288$

Small screen: $A = 10\sqrt{2} \times 10\sqrt{2} = 200$

The visible area of the larger screen is 88 square inches bigger than the visible area of the smaller screen.

6. **10:** If $AD = DB = DC$, then the three triangular regions in this figure are all isosceles triangles. Therefore, you can fill in some of the missing angle measurements as shown to the right. Since you know that there are 180° in the large triangle ABC, you can write the following equation:

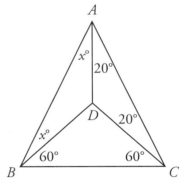

$$x + x + 20 + 20 + 60 + 60 = 180$$
$$2x + 160 = 180$$
$$x = 10$$

7. **7:** If two sides of a triangle are 4 and 10, the third side must be greater than $10 - 4$ and smaller than $10 + 4$. Therefore, the possible values for x are {7, 8, 9, 10, 11, 12, and 13}. You can draw a sketch to convince yourself of this result:

8. **$16\sqrt{3}$:** Draw in the height of the triangle (see figure). If triangle ABC is an equilateral triangle, and ABD is a right triangle, then ABD is a 30–60–90 triangle. Therefore, its sides are in the ratio of 1: $\sqrt{3}$: 2. If the hypotenuse is 8, the short leg is 4, and the long leg is $4\sqrt{3}$. This is the height of triangle ABC. Find the area of triangle ABC with the formula for area of a triangle:

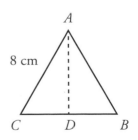

$$A = \frac{b \times h}{2} = \frac{8 \times 4\sqrt{3}}{2} = 16\sqrt{3}$$

Alternatively, you can apply the formula $A = \frac{S^2\sqrt{3}}{4}$, yielding $A = \frac{8^2\sqrt{3}}{4} = \frac{64\sqrt{3}}{4} = 16\sqrt{3}$.

9. **170 inches:** Using the Deluxe Pythagorean Theorem, calculate the length of the diagonal:

$$120^2 + 90^2 + 80^2 = d^2.$$

Note: to make the math easier, drop a zero from each number—but don't forget to add it back in later!

$$12^2 + 9^2 + 8^2 = d^2$$
$$144 + 81 + 64 = d^2$$
$$289 = d^2$$
$$17 = d \qquad\qquad \text{Don't forget to add the zero back in!}$$
$$d = 170 \text{ inches}$$

Alternatively, you can find the diagonal of this rectangular solid by applying the Pythagorean Theorem twice. First, find the diagonal across the bottom of the box:

$$120^2 + 90^2 = c^2$$
$$14{,}400 + 8{,}100 = c^2$$

You might recognize this as a multiple of the common 3–4–5 right triangle.

$$c^2 = 22{,}500$$
$$c = 150$$

Then, find the diagonal of the rectangular box:

$$80^2 + 150^2 = c^2$$
$$6{,}400 + 22{,}500 = c^2$$

You might recognize this as a multiple of the common 8–15–17 right triangle.

$$c^2 = 28{,}900$$
$$c = 170$$

10. **$48\sqrt{3}$ cm²:** You can think of this star as a large equilateral triangle with sides 12 cm long, and three additional smaller equilateral triangles with sides 4 inches long. Using the same 30–60–90 logic you applied in problem #13, you can see that the height of the larger equilateral triangle is $6\sqrt{3}$, and the height of the smaller equilateral triangle is $2\sqrt{3}$. Therefore, the areas of the triangles are as follows:

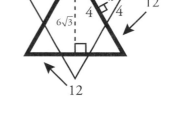

Large triangle: $\qquad A = \frac{b \times h}{2} = \frac{12 \times 6\sqrt{3}}{2} = 36\sqrt{3}$

Small triangles: $\qquad A = \frac{b \times h}{2} = \frac{4 \times 2\sqrt{3}}{2} = 4\sqrt{3}$

The total area of three smaller triangles and one large triangle is:

$$36\sqrt{3} + 3(4\sqrt{3}) = 48\sqrt{3} \text{ cm}^2$$

P

Alternatively, you can apply the formula $A = \dfrac{S^2\sqrt{3}}{4}$.

Large triangle: $A = \dfrac{12^2\sqrt{3}}{4} = \dfrac{144\sqrt{3}}{4} = 36\sqrt{3}$

Small triangle: $A = \dfrac{4^2\sqrt{3}}{4} = \dfrac{16\sqrt{3}}{4} = 4\sqrt{3}$

Then add the area of the large triangle and the area of three smaller triangles, as above.

Chapter 3 *of* Geometry

Circles & Cylinders

In This Chapter...

Chapter 3:
Circles & Cylinders

A circle is defined as the set of points in a plane that are equidistant from a fixed center point. A circle contains 360° (360 degrees).

Any line segment that connects the center point to a point on the circle is termed a **radius** of the circle. If point *O* is the center of the circle shown to the right, then segment *OC* is a radius.

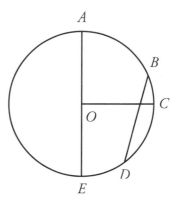

Any line segment that connects two points on a circle is called a **chord**. Any chord that passes through the center of the circle is called a **diameter**. Notice that the diameter is two times the length of the radius. Line segment *BD* is a chord of the circle shown to the right. Line segment *AE* is a diameter of the circle.

The GMAT tests your ability to find (1) the circumference and (2) the area of whole and partial circles. In addition, you must know how to work with cylinders, which are three-dimensional shapes made, in part, of circles. The GMAT tests your ability to find (3) the surface area and (4) the volume of cylinders.

Radius, Diameter, Circumference, and Area

The relationships between these four elements remain constant for every circle.

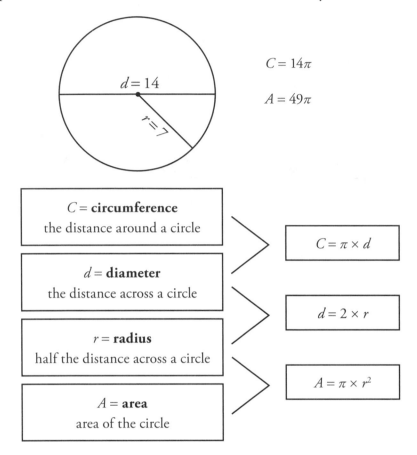

This means that **if you know *any* of these values, you can determine the rest**.

For Problem Solving questions, you should be comfortable using one of these values to solve for the other three. For Data Sufficiency questions, a little information goes a long way. If you know that you are able to solve for each of these values, you do not actually have to perform the calculation.

Revolution = Circumference

A full revolution, or turn, of a spinning wheel is equivalent to the wheel going around once. A point on the edge of the wheel travels one circumference in one revolution. Note also that a full revolution, or turn, of a spinning wheel is equivalent to the wheel going around once. A point on the edge of the wheel travels one circumference in one revolution. For example, if a wheel spins at 3 revolutions per second, a point on the edge travels a distance equal to 3 circumferences per second. If the wheel has a diameter of 4 feet, then the point travels at a rate of $3 \times 4\pi = 12\pi$ feet per second.

Circumference and Arc Length

Often, the GMAT will ask you to solve for a portion of the distance on a circle, instead of the entire circumference. This portion is termed an **arc**. Arc length can be found by determining what fraction the arc is of the entire circumference. This can be done by looking at the central angle that defines the arc.

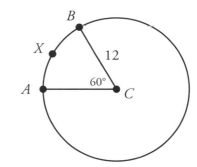

> **What is the length of arc AXB?**

Arc *AXB* is the arc from *A* to *B*, passing through the point *X*. To find its length, first find the circumference of the circle. The radius is given as 12. To find the circumference, use the formula $C = 2\pi r = 2\pi(12) = 24\pi$.

Then, use the central angle to determine what fraction the arc is of the entire circle. Since the arc is defined by the central angle of 60 degrees, and the entire circle is 360 degrees, then the arc is $\dfrac{60}{360} = \dfrac{1}{6}$ of the circle.

Therefore, the measure of arc $AXB = \left(\dfrac{1}{6}\right)(24\pi) = 4\pi$.

Perimeter of a Sector

The boundaries of a **sector** of a circle are formed by the arc and two radii. Think of a sector as a slice of pizza. The arc corresponds to the crust, and the center of the circle corresponds to the tip of the slice.

If you know the length of the radius and the central (or inscribed) angle, you can find the perimeter of the sector.

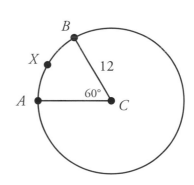

> **What is the perimeter of sector ABC?**

In the previous example, we found the length of arc *AXB* to be 4π. Therefore, the perimeter of the sector is:

$$4\pi + 12 + 12 = 24 + 4\pi.$$

Area of a Circle

The space inside a circle is termed the area of the circle. This area is just like the area of a polygon. Just as with circumference, the only information you need to find the area of a circle is the radius of that circle. The formula for the area of any circle is:

$$A = \pi r^2$$

where A is the area, r is the radius, and π is a number that is approximately 3.14.

What is the area of a circle with a circumference of 16π?

In order to find the area of a circle, all you must know is its radius. If the circumference of the circle is 16π (and $C = 2\pi r$), then the radius must be 8. Plug this into the area formula:

$A = \pi r^2 = \pi(8^2) = 64\pi$.

Area of a Sector

Often, the GMAT will ask you to solve for the area of a sector of a circle, instead of the area of the entire circle. You can find the area of a sector by determining the fraction of the entire area that the sector occupies. To determine this fraction, look at the central angle that defines the sector.

What is the area of sector ACB (the striped region) below?

First, find the area of the entire circle:

$A = \pi r^2 = \pi(3^2) = 9\pi$.

Then, use the central angle to determine what fraction of the entire circle is represented by the sector. Since the sector is defined by the central angle of 60°, and the entire circle is 360°, the sector occupies 60°/360°, or one-sixth, of the area of the circle.

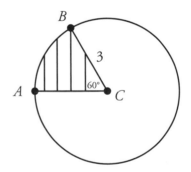

Therefore, the area of sector ACB is $\left(\dfrac{1}{6}\right)(9\pi) = 1.5\pi$.

Inscribed vs. Central Angles

Thus far, in dealing with arcs and sectors, we have referred to the concept of a **central angle**. A central angle is defined as an angle whose vertex lies at the center point of a circle. As we have seen, a central angle defines both an arc and a sector of a circle.

Another type of angle is termed an **inscribed angle**. An inscribed angle has its vertex on the circle itself. The following diagrams illustrate the difference between a central angle and an inscribed angle.

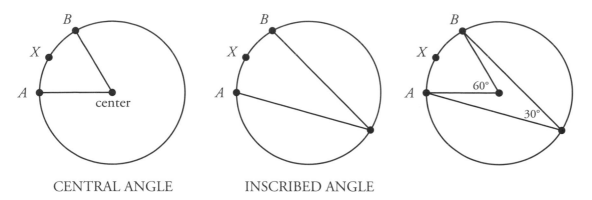

CENTRAL ANGLE   INSCRIBED ANGLE

Notice that, in the circle at the far right, there is a central angle and an inscribed angle, both of which intercept arc *AXB*. It is the central angle that defines the arc. That is, the arc is 60° (or one sixth of the complete 360° circle). **An inscribed angle is equal to half of the arc it intercepts**, in degrees. In this case, the inscribed angle is 30°, which is half of 60°.

Inscribed Triangles

Related to this idea of an inscribed angle is that of an **inscribed triangle**. A triangle is said to be inscribed in a circle if all of the vertices of the triangle are points on the circle. The important rule to remember is: **if one of the sides of an inscribed triangle is a *diameter* of the circle, then the triangle *must* be a right triangle.** Conversely, any right triangle inscribed in a circle must have the diameter of the circle as one of its sides (thereby splitting the circle in half).

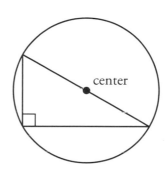

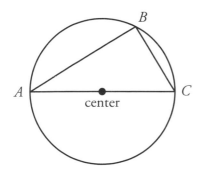

Above right is a special case of the rule mentioned above (that an inscribed angle is equal to half of the arc it intercepts, in degrees). In this case, the right angle (90°) lies opposite a semicircle, which is an arc that measures 180°.

In the inscribed triangle to the left, triangle *ABC* must be a right triangle, since *AC* is a diameter of the circle.

3

Cylinders and Surface Area

Two circles and a rectangle combine to form a three-dimensional shape called a right circular cylinder (referred to from now on simply as a **cylinder**). The top and bottom of the cylinder are circles, while the middle of the cylinder is formed from a rolled-up rectangle, as shown in the diagram below:

In order to determine the surface area of a cylinder, sum the areas of the 3 surfaces: The area of each circle is πr^2, while the area of the rectangle is length × width. Looking at the figures on the left, we can see that the length of the rectangle is equal to the circumference of the circle ($2\pi r$), and the width of the rectangle is equal to the height of the cylinder (h). Therefore, the area of the rectangle is $2\pi r \times h$. To find the total surface area of a cylinder, add the area of the circular top and bottom, as well as the area of the rectangle that wraps around the outside.

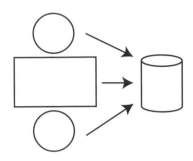

$$SA = 2 \text{ circles} + \text{rectangle} = 2(\pi r^2) + 2\pi rh$$

The only information you need to find the surface area of a cylinder is (1) the radius of the cylinder and (2) the height of the cylinder.

Cylinders and Volume

The volume of a cylinder measures how much "stuff" it can hold inside. In order to find the volume of a cylinder, use the following formula.

$$V = \pi r^2 h$$

V is the volume, r is the radius of the cylinder, and h is the height of the cylinder.

As with finding surface area, determining the volume of a cylinder requires two pieces of information: (1) the radius of the cylinder and (2) the height of the cylinder.

The diagram below shows that two cylinders can have the same volume but different shapes (and therefore each fits differently inside a larger object).

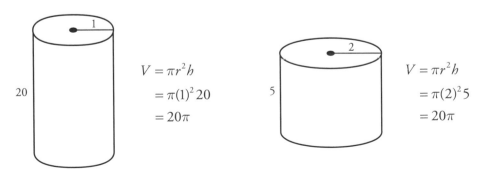

Problem Set (Note: Figures are not drawn to scale.)

1.   A cylinder has a surface area of 360π, and is 3 units tall. What is the diameter of the cylinder's circular base?

2.   Randy can run π meters every 2 seconds. If the circular track has a radius of 75 meters, how many minutes does it take Randy to run twice around the track?

3.   A circular lawn with a radius of 5 meters is surrounded by a circular walkway that is 4 meters wide (see figure). What is the area of the walkway?

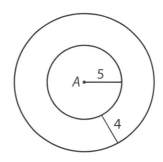

4.   A cylindrical water tank has a diameter of 14 meters and a height of 20 meters. A water truck can fill π cubic meters of the tank every minute. How long will it take the water truck to fill the water tank from empty to half-full?

5.   *BE* and *CD* are both diameters of circle with center A (see figure). If the area of Circle A is 180 units^2, what is the area of sector *ABC* + sector *ADE*?

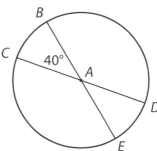

6.   Jane has to paint a cylindrical column that is 14 feet high and that has a circular base with a radius of 3 feet. If one bucket of paint will cover 10π square feet, how many full buckets does Jane need to buy in order to paint the column, including the top and bottom?

7.   If angle *ABC* is 40 degrees (see figure), and the area of the circle is 81π, how long is arc *AXC*? *CB* is a diameter of the circle.

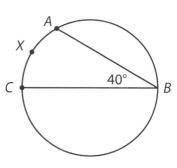

8.   A Hydrogenator water gun has a cylindrical water tank, which is 30 centimeters long. Using a hose, Jack fills his Hydrogenator with π cubic centimeters of his water tank every second. If it takes him 8 minutes to fill the tank with water, what is the diameter of the circular base of the gun's water tank?

Solutions

1. **24:** The surface area of a cylinder is the area of the circular top and bottom, plus the area of its wrapped-around rectangular third face. You can express this in formula form as:

$$SA = 2(\pi r^2) + 2\pi rh$$

Substitute the known values into this formula to find the radius of the circular base:

$$360\pi = 2(\pi r^2) + 2\pi r(3)$$
$$360\pi = 2\pi r^2 + 6\pi r$$
$$r^2 + 3r - 180 = 0$$
$$(r + 15)(r - 12) = 0$$

$$r + 15 = 0 \qquad OR \qquad r - 12 = 0$$
$$r = \{-15, 12\}$$

Use only the positive value of r: 12. If $r = 12$, the diameter of the cylinder's circular base is 24.

2. **10 minutes:** The distance around the track is the circumference of the circle:

$$C = 2\pi r$$
$$= 150\pi$$

Running twice around the circle would equal a distance of 300π meters. If Randy can run π meters every 2 seconds, he runs 30π meters every minute. Therefore, it will take him 10 minutes to run around the circular track twice.

3. **$56\pi\,\text{m}^2$:** The area of the walkway is the area of the entire image (walkway + lawn) minus the area of the lawn. To find the area of each circle, use the formula:

Large circle: $A = \pi r^2 = \pi(9)^2 = 81\pi$
Small circle: $A = \pi r^2 = \pi(5)^2 = 25\pi$ $\qquad\qquad\qquad 81\pi - 25\pi = 56\pi\,\text{m}^2$

4. **490 minutes, or 8 hours and 10 minutes:** First find the volume of the cylindrical tank:

$$V = \pi r^2 \times h$$
$$= \pi(7)^2 \times 20$$
$$= 980\pi$$

If the water truck can fill π cubic meters of the tank every minute, it will take 980 minutes to fill the tank completely; therefore, it will take $980 \div 2 = 490$ minutes to fill the tank halfway. This is equal to 8 hours and 10 minutes.

5. **40 units²:** The two central angles, *CAB* and *DAE*, describe a total of 80°. Simplify the fraction to find out what fraction of the circle this represents:

$$\frac{80}{360} = \frac{2}{9} \qquad \frac{2}{9} \text{ of 180 units}^2 \text{ is 40 units}^2.$$

6. **11 buckets:** The surface area of a cylinder is the area of the circular top and bottom, plus the area of its wrapped-around rectangular third face.

Top & Bottom: $A = \pi r^2 = 9\pi$
Rectangle: $A = 2\pi r \times h = 84\pi$

The total surface area, then, is $9\pi + 9\pi + 84\pi = 102\pi$ ft². If one bucket of paint will cover 10π ft², then Jane will need 10.2 buckets to paint the entire column. Since paint stores do not sell fractional buckets, she will need to purchase 11 buckets.

7. **4π:** If the area of the circle is 81π, then the radius of the circle is 9 ($A = \pi r^2$). Therefore, the total circumference of the circle is 18π ($C = 2\pi r$). Angle *ABC*, an inscribed angle of 40°, corresponds to a central angle of 80°. Thus, arc *AXC* is equal to $\frac{80}{360} = \frac{2}{9}$ of the total circumference:

$$\frac{2}{9}(18\pi) = 4\pi.$$

8. **8 cm:** In 8 minutes, or 480 seconds, 480π cm³ of water flows into the tank. Therefore, the volume of the tank is 480π. You are given a height of 30, so you can solve for the radius:

$$V = \pi r^2 \times h$$
$$480\pi = 30\pi r^2$$
$$r^2 = 16$$
$$r = 4$$

Therefore, the diameter of the tank's base is 8 cm.

Chapter 4
of Geometry

Lines & Angles

In This Chapter...

Chapter 4:

Lines & Angles

A straight line is the shortest distance between 2 points. As an angle, a line measures 180°.

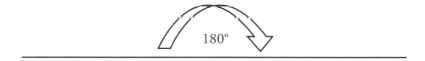

Parallel lines are lines that lie in a plane and that never intersect. No matter how far you extend the lines, they never meet. Two parallel lines are shown below:

Perpendicular lines are lines that intersect at a 90° angle. Two perpendicular lines are shown below:

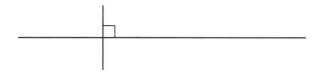

There are two major line-angle relationships that you must know for the GMAT:

 (1) The angles formed by any intersecting lines.
 (2) The angles formed by parallel lines cut by a transversal.

Intersecting Lines

4

Intersecting lines have three important properties.

First, the interior angles formed by intersecting lines form a circle, so the sum of these angles is 360°. In the diagram shown, $a + b + c + d = 360$.

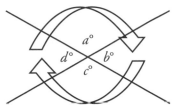

Second, interior angles that combine to form a line sum to 180°. These are termed **supplementary angles**. Thus, in the diagram shown, $a + b = 180$, because angles a and b form a line together. Other supplementary angles are $b + c = 180$, $c + d = 180$, and $d + a = 180$.

Third, angles found opposite each other where these two lines intersect are equal. These are called **vertical angles**. Thus, in the diagram above, $a = c$, because both of these angles are opposite each other, and are formed from the same two lines. Additionally, $b = d$ for the same reason.

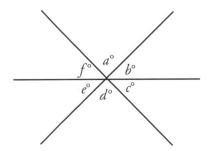

Note that these rules apply to more than two lines that intersect at a point, as shown to the left. In this diagram, $a + b + c + d + e + f = 360$, because these angles combine to form a circle. In addition, $a + b + c = 180$, because these three angles combine to form a line. Finally, $a = d$, $b = e$, and $c = f$, because they are pairs of vertical angles.

Exterior Angles of a Triangle

An **exterior angle** of a triangle is equal in measure to the sum of the two non-adjacent (opposite) **interior angles** of the triangle. For example:

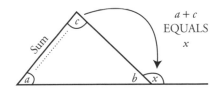

$a + b + c = 180$ (sum of angles in a triangle).
$b + x = 180$ (supplementary angles).
Therefore, $x = a + c$.

This property is frequently tested on the GMAT! In particular, look for exterior angles within more complicated diagrams. You might even redraw the diagram with certain lines removed to isolate the triangle and exterior angle you need.

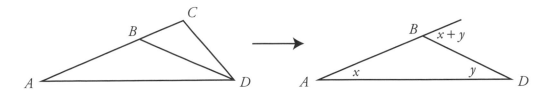

Parallel Lines Cut By a Transversal

The GMAT makes frequent use of diagrams that include parallel lines cut by a **transversal**.

Notice that there are 8 angles formed by this construction, but there are only *two* different angle measures (*a* and *b*). All the **acute** angles (less than 90°) in this diagram are equal. Likewise, all the **obtuse** angles (more than 90° but less than 180°) are equal. Any acute angle is supplementary to any obtuse angle. Thus, *a* + *b* = 180°.

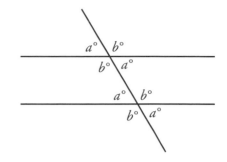

When you see a transversal cutting two lines that you know to be parallel, fill in all the *a* (acute) and *b* (obtuse) angles, just as in the diagram above.

Sometimes the GMAT disguises the parallel lines and the transversal so that they are not readily apparent, as in the diagram pictured to the right. In these disguised cases, it is a good idea to extend the lines so that you can easily see the parallel lines and the transversal. Just remember always to be on the lookout for parallel lines. When you see them, extend lines and label the acute and obtuse angles. You might also mark the parallel lines with arrows, as shown below to the right.

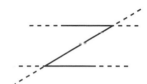

The GMAT uses the symbol ‖ to indicate in text that two lines or line segments are parallel. For instance, if you see *MN* ‖ *OP* in a problem, you know that line segment *MN* is parallel to line segment *OP*.

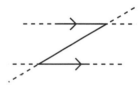

Problem Set

Problems 1–2 refer to the diagram to the right, where line *AB* is parallel to line *CD*.

1.   If $x - y = 10$, what is x?

2.   If $x + (x + y) = 320$, what is x?

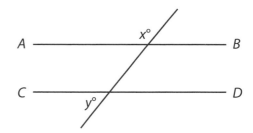

Problems 3–4 refer to the diagram to the right.

3.   If a is 95, what is $b + d - e$?

4.   If $c + f = 70$, and $d = 80$, what is b?

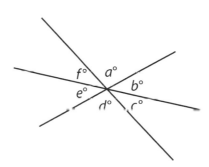

Problems 5–7 refer to the diagram to the right.

5.   If $c + g = 140$, find k.

6.   If $g = 90$, what is $a + k$?

7.   If $f + k = 150$, find b.

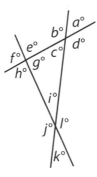

Solutions

1. 95: You know that $x + y = 180$, since any acute angle formed by a transversal that cuts across two parallel lines is supplementary to any obtuse angle. Use the information given to set up a system of two equations with two variables:

$$\begin{aligned} x + y &= 180 \\ x - y &= 10 \\ \hline 2x &= 190 \\ x &= 95 \end{aligned}$$

2. 140: Use the fact that $x + y = 180$ to set up a system of two equations with two variables:

$$x + y = 180 \quad \longrightarrow \quad \begin{aligned} -x - y &= -180 \\ +\;\; 2x + y &= 320 \\ \hline x &= 140 \end{aligned}$$

Alternatively, because you know that $x + y = 180$, substitute this into the given equation of $x + (x + y) = 320$ to solve for x:

$$\begin{aligned} x + 180 &= 320 \\ x &= 140 \end{aligned}$$

3. 95: Because a and d are vertical angles, they have the same measure: $a = d = 95°$. Likewise, since b and e are vertical angles, they have the same measure: $b = e$. Therefore, $b + d - e = b + d - b = d = 95°$.

4. 65: Because c and f are vertical angles, they have the same measure: $c + f = 70$, so $c = f = 35$. Notice that b, c, and d form a straight line: $b + c + d = 180$. Substitute the known values of c and d into this equation:

$$\begin{aligned} b + 35 + 80 &= 180 \\ b + 115 &= 180 \\ b &= 65 \end{aligned}$$

5. 40: If $c + g = 140$, then $i = 40$, because there are $180°$ in a triangle. Since k is vertical to i, k is also $= 40$. Alternately, if $c + g = 140$, then $j = 140$, since j is an exterior angle of the triangle and is therefore equal to the sum of the two remote interior angles. Since k is supplementary to j, $k = 180 - 140 = 40$.

6. 90: If $g = 90$, then the other two angles in the triangle, c and i, sum to 90. Since a and k are vertical angles to c and i, they sum to 90 as well.

7. 150: Angles f and k are vertical to angles g and i. These two angles, then, must also sum to 150. Angle b, an exterior angle of the triangle, must be equal to the sum of the two remote interior angles g and i. Therefore, $b = 150$.

Alternatively, $f = g$ and $k = I$, so $g + I = 150$. Therefore, $c = 30$. Because $c + b = 180$, $30 + b = 180$, and $b = 150$.

Chapter 5 *of* Geometry

Coordinate Plane

In This Chapter. . .

The Slope of a Line

The 4 Types of Slopes

The Intercepts of a Line

Slope-Intercept Equation: $y = mx + b$

Horizontal and Vertical Lines

Step by Step: From 2 Points to a Line

The Distance Between 2 Points

Positive and Negative Quadrants

Chapter 5:
Coordinate Plane

The coordinate plane is formed by a horizontal axis or reference line (the "**x-axis**") and a vertical axis (the "**y-axis**"), as shown here. These axes are each marked off like a number line, with both positive and negative numbers. The axes cross at right angles at the number zero on both axes.

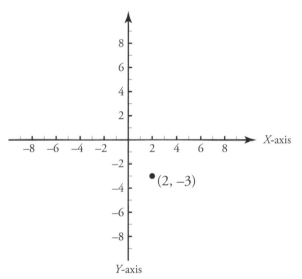

Points in the plane are identified by using an ordered pair of numbers, such as the one to the left: (2, −3). The first number in the ordered pair (2) is the **x-coordinate**, which corresponds to the point's horizontal location, as measured by the *x*-axis. The second number in the ordered pair (−3) is the **y-coordinate**, which corresponds to the point's vertical location, as indicated by the *y*-axis. The point (0, 0), where the axes cross, is called the **origin**.

A line in the plane is formed by the connection of two or more points. Notice that along the *x*-axis, the *y*-coordinate is zero. Likewise, along the *y*-axis, the *x*-coordinate is zero.

If the GMAT gives you coordinates with other variables, just match them to *x* and *y*. For instance, if you have point (*a*, *b*), *a* is the *x*-coordinate and *b* is the *y*-coordinate.

The Slope of a Line

The slope of a line is defined as "rise over run"—that is, how much the line *rises* vertically divided by how much the line *runs* horizontally.

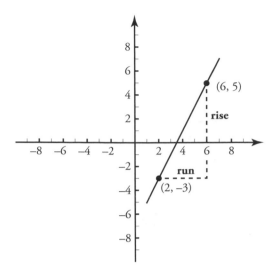

The slope of a line can be determined by taking any two points on the line and (1) determining the "rise," or difference between their *y*-coordinates and (2) determining the "run," or difference between their *x*-coordinates.

The slope is simply $\dfrac{\text{rise}}{\text{run}}$.

For example, in the diagram at the right, the line rises vertically from −3 to 5. This distance can be found by subtracting the *y*-coordinates: 5 − (−3) = 8. Thus, the line rises 8 units. The line also runs horizontally from 2 to 6. This distance can be found by subtracting the *x*-coordinates: 6 − 2 = 4. Thus, the line runs 4 units.

When you put together these results, you see that the slope of the line is: $\dfrac{\text{rise}}{\text{run}} = \dfrac{8}{4} = 2$.

Two other points on the line would typically have a different rise and run, but the slope would be the same. The "rise over run" would always be 2. A line has a constant slope.

The 4 Types of Slopes

There are four types of slopes that a line can have:

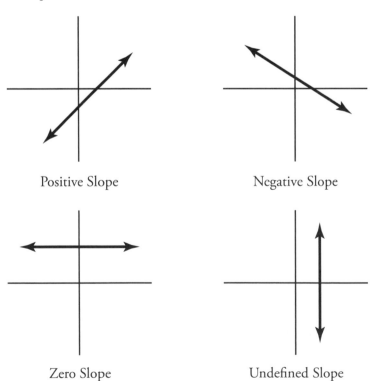

Positive Slope   Negative Slope

Zero Slope   Undefined Slope

A line with positive slope rises upward from left to right. A line with negative slope falls downward from left to right. A horizontal line has zero slope. A vertical line has undefined slope. Notice that the *x*-axis has zero slope, while the *y*-axis has undefined slope.

The Intercepts of a Line

A point where a line intersects a coordinate axis is called an **intercept**. There are two types of intercepts: the *x*-intercept, where the line intersects the *x*-axis, and the *y*-intercept, where the line intersects the *y*-axis.

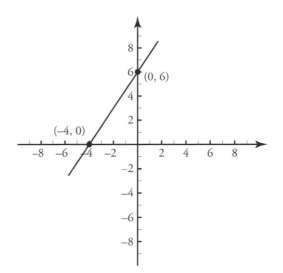

The *x*-intercept is expressed using the ordered pair $(x, 0)$, where *x* is the point where the line intersects the *x*-axis. **The *x*-intercept is the point on the line at which $y = 0$.** In this diagram, the *x*-intercept is −4, as expressed by the ordered pair (−4, 0).

The *y*-intercept is expressed using the ordered pair $(0, y)$, where y is the point where the line intersects the *y*-axis. **The *y*-intercept is the point on the line at which $x = 0$.** In this diagram, the *y*-intercept is 6, as expressed by the ordered pair (0, 6).

To find *x*-intercepts, **plug in 0 for *y*.** To find *y*-intercepts, **plug in 0 for *x*.**

Slope-Intercept Equation: *y* = m*x* + b

All lines can be written as equations in the form $y = mx + b$, where m represents the slope of the line and b represents the *y*-intercept of the line. This is a convenient form for graphing.

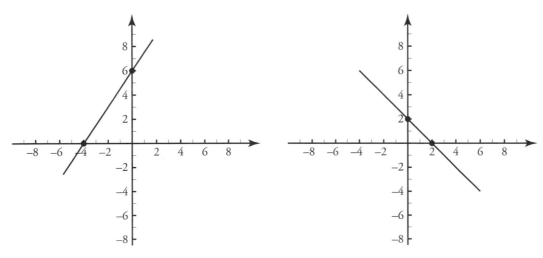

Linear equations represent lines in the coordinate plane. Linear equations often look like this: Ax + By = C, where A, B, and C are numbers. For instance, $6x + 3y = 18$ is a linear equation. Linear equations never involve terms such as x^2, $\sqrt{x}$, or xy. When you want to graph a linear equation, rewrite it in the slope-intercept form ($y = mx + b$). Then you can easily draw the line.

What is the slope-intercept form for a line with the equation $6x + 3y = 18$?

Rewrite the equation by solving for y as follows:

$$6x + 3y = 18$$
$$3y = 18 - 6x \qquad \text{Subtract } 6x \text{ from both sides}$$
$$y = 6 - 2x \qquad \text{Divide both sides by 3}$$
$$y = -2x + 6 \qquad \text{Thus, the } y\text{-intercept is } (0, 6), \text{ and the slope is } -2.$$

Horizontal and Vertical Lines

Horizontal and vertical lines are not expressed in the $y = mx + b$ form. Instead, they are expressed as simple, one-variable equations.

Horizontal lines are expressed in the form:
$y = $ *some number*, such as $y = 3$ or $y = 5$.

Vertical lines are expressed in the form:
$x = $ *some number*, such as $x = 4$ or $x = 7$.

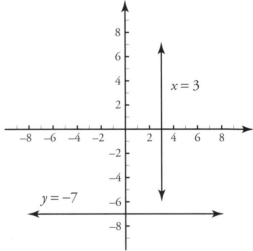

All the points on a vertical line have the same x-coordinate. This is why the equation of a vertical line is defined only by x. The y-axis itself corresponds to the equation $x = 0$. Likewise, all the points on a horizontal line have the same y-coordinate. This is why the equation of a horizontal line is defined only by y. The x-axis itself corresponds to the equation $y = 0$.

Step by Step: From 2 Points to a Line

If you are given any two points on a line, you should be able to write an equation for that line in the form $y = mx + b$. Here is the step-by-step method:

Find the equation of the line containing the points (5, –2) and (3, 4).

<u>FIRST</u>: Find the slope of the line by calculating the rise over the run.

The rise is the difference between the *y*-coordinates, while the run is the difference between the *x*-coordinates. The sign of each difference is important, so subtract the *x*-coordinates and the *y*-coordinates in the same order.

$$\frac{\text{rise}}{\text{run}} = \frac{y_1 - y_2}{x_1 - x_2} = \frac{-2 - 4}{5 - 3} = \frac{-6}{2} = -3 \qquad \text{The slope of the line is } -3.$$

SECOND: Plug the slope in for m in the slope-intercept equation.

$$y = -3x + b$$

THIRD: Solve for b, the *y*-intercept, by plugging the coordinates of one point into the equation. Either point's coordinates will work.

Plugging the point (3, 4) into the equation (3 for *x* and 4 for *y*) yields the following:

$$4 = -3(3) + b$$
$$4 - -9 + b \qquad\qquad \text{The } y\text{-intercept of the line is 13.}$$
$$b = 13$$

FOURTH: Write the equation in the form $y = mx + b$.

$$y = -3x + 13 \qquad\qquad \text{This is the equation of the line.}$$

Note that sometimes the GMAT will only give you one point on the line, along with the *y*-intercept. This is the same thing as giving you two points on the line, because the *y*-intercept is a point! A *y*-intercept of 4 is the same as the ordered pair (0, 4).

The Distance Between 2 Points

The distance between any two points in the coordinate plane can be calculated by using the Pythagorean Theorem. For example:

   What is the distance between the points (1, 3) and (7, −5)?

(1) Draw a right triangle connecting the points.

(2) Find the lengths of the two legs of the triangle by calculating the rise and the run.

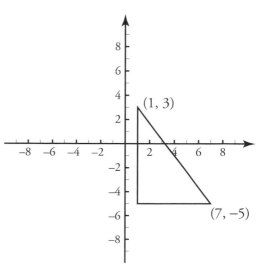

   The *y*-coordinate changes from 3 to −5, a difference of 8 (the vertical leg).

   The *x*-coordinate changes from 1 to 7, a difference of 6 (the horizontal leg).

(3) Use the Pythagorean Theorem to calculate the length of the diagonal, which is the distance between the points.

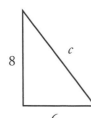

$$6^2 + 8^2 = c^2$$
$$36 + 64 = c^2$$
$$100 = c^2$$
$$c = 10$$

The distance between the two points is 10 units.

Alternatively, to find the hypotenuse, you might have recognized this triangle as a variation of a 3–4–5 triangle (specifically, a 6–8–10 triangle).

Positive and Negative Quadrants

There are four quadrants in the coordinate plane, as shown in the diagram below.

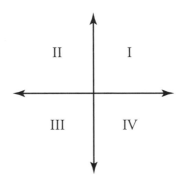

Quadrant I contains only those points with a **positive** x-coordinate & a **positive** y-coordinate.

Quadrant II contains only those points with a **negative** x-coordinate & a **positive** y-coordinate.

Quadrant III contains only those points with a **negative** x-coordinate & a **negative** y-coordinate.

Quadrant IV contains only those points with a **positive** x-coordinate & a **negative** y-coordinate.

The GMAT sometimes asks you to determine which quadrants a given line passes through. For example:

Which quadrants does the line $2x + y = 5$ pass through?

(1) First, rewrite the line in the form $y = mx + b$.

$$2x + y = 5$$
$$y = 5 - 2x$$
$$y = -2x + 5$$

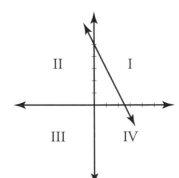

(2) Then sketch the line. Since $b = 5$, the y-intercept is the point (0, 5). The slope is −2, so the line slopes downward steeply to the right from the y-intercept. Although you do not know exactly where the line intersects the x-axis, you can now see that the line passes through quadrants I, II, and IV.

Alternatively, you can find two points on the line by setting x and y equal to zero in the original equation. In this way, you can find the x- and y-intercepts.

$$
\begin{array}{ll}
x = 0 & y = 0 \\
2x + y = 5 & 2x + y = 5 \\
2(0) + y = 5 & 2x + (0) = 5 \\
\qquad y = 5 & \qquad x = 2.5
\end{array}
$$

The points $(0, 5)$ and $(2.5, 0)$ are both on the line.

Now sketch the line, using the points you have identified. If you plot $(0, 5)$ and $(2.5, 0)$ on the coordinate plane, you can connect them to see the position of the line. Again, the line passes through quadrants I, II, and IV.

5

Problem Set

1. A line has the equation $y = 3x + 7$. At which point will this line intersect the y-axis?

2. A line has the equation $x = \dfrac{y}{80} - 20$. At which point will this line intersect the x-axis?

3. A line has the equation $x = -2y + z$. If (3, 2) is a point on the line, what is z?

4. A line has a slope of $\dfrac{1}{6}$ and intersects the x-axis at (−24, 0). Where does this line intersect the y-axis?

5. A line has a slope of $\dfrac{3}{4}$ and intersects the point (−12, −39). At which point does this line intersect the x-axis?

6. Which quadrants, if any, do not contain any points on the line represented by $x - y = 18$?

7. Which quadrants, if any, do not contain any points on the line represented by $x = 10y$?

8. Which quadrants, if any, contain points on the line represented by $x + 18 = 2y$?

P

Solutions

1. **(0, 7):** A line intersects the y-axis at the y-intercept. Since this equation is written in slope-intercept form, the y-intercept is easy to identify: 7. Thus, the line intersects the y-axis at the point (0, 7).

2. **(–20, 0):** A line intersects the x-axis at the x-intercept, or when the y-coordinate is equal to zero. Substitute zero for y and solve for x:

$$x = 0 - 20$$
$$x = -20$$

3. **7:** Substitute the coordinates (3, 2) for x and y and solve for z:

$$3 = -2(2) + z$$
$$3 = -4 + z$$
$$z = 7$$

4. **(0, 4):** Use the information given to find the equation of the line:

$$y = \frac{1}{6}x + b$$
$$0 = \frac{1}{6}(-24) + b$$
$$0 = -4 + b$$
$$b = 4$$

The variable b represents the y-intercept. Therefore, the line intersects the y-axis at (0, 4).

5. **(40, 0):** Use the information given to find the equation of the line:

$$y = \frac{3}{4}x + b$$
$$-39 = \frac{3}{4}(-12) + b$$
$$-39 = -9 + b$$
$$b = -30$$

The line intersects the x-axis when $y = 0$. Set y equal to zero and solve for x:

$$0 = \frac{3}{4}x - 30$$
$$\frac{3}{4}x = 30$$
$$x = 40$$

The line intersects the *x*-axis at (40, 0).

6. **II:** First, rewrite the line in slope-intercept form:

$$y = x - 18$$

Find the intercepts by setting *x* to zero and *y* to zero:

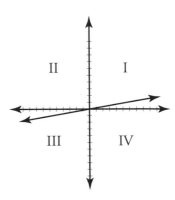

$$y = 0 - 18 \qquad\qquad\qquad 0 = x - 18$$
$$y = -18 \qquad\qquad\qquad\quad x = 18$$

Plot the points: (0, −18), and (18, 0). From the sketch, you can see that the line does not pass through quadrant II.

7. **II and IV:** First, rewrite the line in slope-intercept form:

$$y = \frac{x}{10}$$

Notice from the equation that the *y*-intercept of the line is (0,0). This means that the line crosses the *y*-intercept at the origin, so the *x*- and *y*-intercepts are the same. To find another point on the line, substitute any convenient number for *x*; in this case, 10 would be a convenient, or "smart," number.

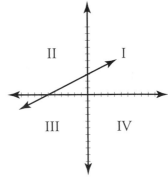

$$y = \frac{10}{10} = 1 \qquad\qquad \text{The point (10, 1) is on the line.}$$

Plot the points: (0, 0) and (10, 1). From the sketch, you can see that the line does not pass through quadrants II and IV.

8. **I, II, and III:** First, rewrite the line in slope-intercept form:

$$y = \frac{x}{2} + 9$$

Find the intercepts by setting *x* to zero and *y* to zero:

$$0 = \frac{x}{2} + 9 \qquad\qquad\qquad y = \frac{0}{2} + 9$$
$$x = -18 \qquad\qquad\qquad\qquad y = 9$$

Plot the points: (−18, 0) and (0, 9). From the sketch, you can see that the line passes through quadrants I, II, and III.

MANHATTAN
GMAT

Chapter 6 *of* Geometry

Geometry Strategies

In This Chapter...

Chapter 6:
Geometry Strategies

The following five sections appear in all 5 quant strategy guides. If you are familiar with this information, skip ahead to page 90 for new content.

Data Sufficiency Basics

Every Data Sufficiency problem has the *same* basic form:

> The **Question Stem** is (sometimes) made up of two parts:
>
> (1) The **Question**: *"What day of the week is the party on?"*
> (2) Possible **Additional Info**: *"Jon's birthday party is this week."*
>   This might simply be background OR could provide additional constraints or equations needed to solve the problem.

Jon's birthday party is this week. What day of the week is the party on?

(1)   The party is not on Monday or Tuesday.
(2)   The party is not on Wednesday, Thursday, or Friday.

(A)   Statement (1) ALONE is sufficient, but statement (2) is NOT sufficient
(B)   Statement (2) ALONE is sufficient, but statement (1) is NOT sufficient
(C)   BOTH statements TOGETHER are sufficient, but NEITHER statement ALONE is sufficient
(D)   EACH statement ALONE is sufficient
(E)   Statements (1) and (2) TOGETHER are NOT sufficient

> Following the question are **two Statements** labeled (1) and (2).
>
> To answer Data Sufficiency problems correctly, you need to decide **whether the statements provide enough information to answer the question**. In other words, do you have *sufficient data*?

> Lastly, we are given the **Answer Choices**.
>
> These are the *same* for every Data Sufficiency problem so **memorize them** as soon as possible.

What Does "Sufficient" Mean?

The key to Data Sufficiency is to remember that it *does not* require you to answer the question asked in the question stem. Instead, you need to decide whether the statements provide enough information to answer the question.

Notice that in answer choices (A), (B), and (D), you are asked to evaluate each of the statements separately. You must then decide if the information given in each is sufficient (on its own) to answer the question in the stem.

The correct answer choice will be:

> **(A)** when Statement (1) provides enough information by itself, but Statement (2) does not,
>
> **(B)** when Statement (2) provides enough information by itself, but Statement (1) does not,
>
> OR
>
> **(D)** when BOTH statements, *independently*, provide enough information.

But what happens when you cannot answer the question with *either* statement individually? Now you must put them together and decide if all of the information given is sufficient to answer the question in the stem.

If you **must** use the statements together, the correct answer choice will be:

> **(C)** if together they provide enough information (but neither alone is sufficient),
>
> OR
>
> **(E)** if the statements, even together, do not provide enough information.

We will revisit the answer choices when we discuss a basic process for Data Sufficiency.

The DS Process

Data Sufficiency tests logical reasoning as much as it tests mathematical concepts. In order to master Data Sufficiency, develop a consistent process that will help you stay on task. It is very easy to forget what you are actually trying to accomplish as you answer these questions.

To give yourself the best chance of consistently answering DS questions correctly, you need to be methodical. The following steps can help reduce errors on every DS problem.

Step 1: Separate *additional info* from the *actual question*.

If the additional information contains *constraints* or *equations*, make a note on your scrap paper.

Step 2: Determine whether the question is Value or Yes/No.

Value: The **question** asks for the value of an unknown (e.g., What is *x*?).

> A statement is **Sufficient** when it provides **1 possible value**.
> A statement is **Not Sufficient** when it provides **more than 1 possible value**.

Yes/No: The **question** that is asked has two possible answers: Yes or No (e.g., Is *x* even?).

> A statement is **Sufficient** when it provides a **definite Yes or definite No**.
> A statement is **Not Sufficient** when the answer **could be Yes or No**.

	Sufficient	Not Sufficient
Value	**1 Value**	**More than 1 Value**
Yes/No	**1 Answer (Yes or No)**	**More than 1 Answer (Yes AND No)**

Step 3: Decide *exactly* what the question is asking.

To properly evaluate the statements, you must have a very precise understanding of the question asked in the question stem. Ask yourself two questions:

1. What, *precisely*, would be *sufficient*?
2. What, *precisely*, would *not* be *sufficient*?

For instance, suppose the question is, "What is *x*?"

1. What, precisely, would be sufficient? **One value for *x*** (e.g., *x* = 5).
2. What, precisely, would not be sufficient? **More than one value for *x*** (e.g., *x* is prime).

Step 4: Use the Grid to evaluate the statements.

The answer choices need to be evaluated in the proper order. The Grid is a simple but effective tool to help you keep track of your progress. Write the following on your page:

AD
BCE

The two columns below will tell you how to work through the Grid:

First, **evaluate Statement (1)**.

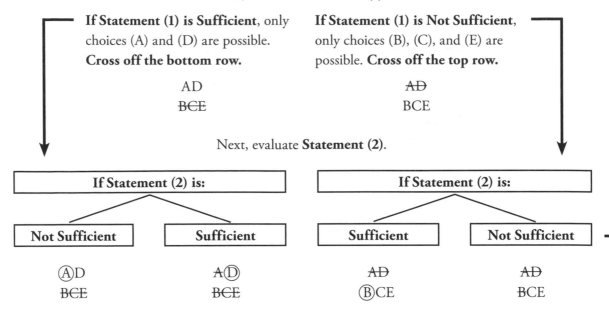

If Statement (1) is Sufficient, only choices (A) and (D) are possible. **Cross off the bottom row.**

AD
~~BCE~~

If Statement (1) is Not Sufficient, only choices (B), (C), and (E) are possible. **Cross off the top row.**

~~AD~~
BCE

Next, evaluate **Statement (2)**.

If Statement (2) is:		If Statement (2) is:	
Not Sufficient	**Sufficient**	**Sufficient**	**Not Sufficient**
Ⓐ D	A Ⓓ	~~AD~~	~~AD~~
~~BCE~~	~~BCE~~	Ⓑ CE	BCE

Notice that the first two steps are always the same: evaluate Statement (1) then evaluate Statement (2).

If neither Statement by itself is sufficient, then the only two possible answers are (C) and (E). The next step is to look at the Statements TOGETHER:

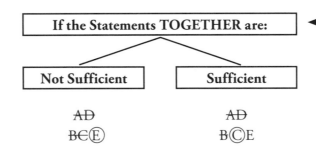

If the Statements TOGETHER are:	
Not Sufficient	**Sufficient**
~~AD~~	~~AD~~
~~BC~~ Ⓔ	~~B~~ Ⓒ ~~E~~

Putting It All Together

Now that you know the process, it's time to work through the practice problem start to finish.

Jon's birthday party is this week. What day of the week is the party on?

(1) The party is not on Monday or Tuesday.
(2) The party is not on Wednesday, Thursday, or Friday.

(A) Statement (1) ALONE is sufficient, but statement (2) is NOT sufficient
(B) Statement (2) ALONE is sufficient, but statement (1) is NOT sufficient
(C) BOTH statements TOGETHER are sufficient, but NEITHER statement ALONE is sufficient
(D) EACH statement ALONE is sufficient
(E) Statements (1) and (2) TOGETHER are NOT sufficient

Step 1: Separate *additional info* from the *actual question*.

Question	Additional Info
What day of the week is the party on?	Jon's birthday party is this week.

Step 2: Determine whether the question is Value or Yes/No.

You need to know the exact day of the week that the party is on.

This is a Value question.

Step 3: Decide *exactly* what the question is asking.

What, precisely, would be sufficient? **One possible day of the week.**
What, precisely, would not be sufficient? **More than one possible day of the week.**

Step 4: Use the Grid to evaluate the statements.

Evaluate Statement (1): Statement (1) tells you that the party is *not* on Monday or Tuesday. The party could still be on Wednesday, Thursday, Friday, Saturday, or Sunday. Statement (1) is Not Sufficient.

~~AD~~
BCE

Evaluate Statement (2): Statement (2) tells you that the party is *not* on Wednesday, Thursday, or Friday. The party could still be on Saturday, Sunday, Monday, or Tuesday. Statement (2) is Not Sufficient.

~~AD~~
~~BCE~~

MANHATTAN
GMAT

Now that you've verified neither statement is sufficient on its own, it's time to evaluate the statements taken together.

Evaluate (1) AND (2): Taking both statements together, we know the party is not on Monday, Tuesday, Wednesday, Thursday, or Friday. The party could still be on Saturday or Sunday. Statements (1) and (2) together are Not Sufficient.

~~AD~~
~~BC~~(E)

The correct answer is **(E)**.

Putting It All Together (Again)

Now try a different, but related, question:

> It rains all day every Saturday and Sunday in Seattle, and never on any other day.
> Is it raining in Seattle right now?
>
> (1) Today is not Monday or Tuesday.
> (2) Today is not Wednesday, Thursday, or Friday.

(A) Statement (1) ALONE is sufficient, but statement (2) is NOT sufficient

(B) Statement (2) ALONE is sufficient, but statement (1) is NOT sufficient

(C) BOTH statements TOGETHER are sufficient, but NEITHER statement ALONE is sufficient

(D) EACH statement ALONE is sufficient

(E) Statements (1) and (2) TOGETHER are NOT sufficient

The statements are exactly the same as in the previous example, but the question has changed. The process is still the same.

Step 1: Separate *additional info* from the *actual question*.

Question	Additional Info
Is it raining in Seattle right now?	It rains all day every Saturday and Sunday in Seattle, and never on any other day.

Step 2: Determine whether the question is Value or Yes/No.

There are two possible answers to this question:

1. Yes, it is raining in Seattle right now.
2. No, it is not raining in Seattle right now.

This is a Yes/No question.

Step 3: Decide *exactly* what the question is asking.

Be careful. This part of the process is usually more complicated when the question is Yes/No. Sufficient is defined as providing a definite answer to the Yes/No question. Since the statements often allow for multiple possible values, you have to ask the Yes/No question for all the possible values.

Before you look at the statements, keep in mind there are only 7 days of the week. You know the answer to the question on each of those days as well. If today is Saturday or Sunday, the answer is **yes, it is raining in Seattle right now**. If today is Monday, Tuesday, Wednesday, Thursday, or Friday, the answer is **no, it is not raining in Seattle right now**.

What, precisely, would be sufficient? **It is definitely raining (Saturday or Sunday) OR it is definitely NOT raining (Monday through Friday).**

What, precisely, would not be sufficient? **It may be raining (e.g., Today is either Friday or Saturday).**

Step 4: Use the Grid to evaluate the statements.

Evaluate Statement (1): Statement (1) tells you that today is *not* Monday or Tuesday. Today could still be Wednesday, Thursday, Friday, Saturday, or Sunday. It might be raining in Seattle right now. You cannot know for sure. Statement (1) is Not Sufficient.

> A̶D̶
> BCE

Evaluate Statement (2): Statement (2) tells you that today is *not* Wednesday, Thursday, or Friday. Today could still be Saturday, Sunday, Monday, or Tuesday. It might be raining in Seattle right now. You cannot know for sure. Statement (2) is Not Sufficient.

> A̶D̶
> B̶CE

Now that you've verified neither statement is sufficient on its own, it's time to evaluate the statement taken together.

Evaluate (1) AND (2): Taking both statements together, you know that today is not Monday, Tuesday, Wednesday, Thursday, or Friday. Today could still be on Saturday or Sunday. If today is Saturday, you know that it is raining in Seattle. If today is Sunday, you know that it is raining in Seattle. Either way, you can say definitely that **yes, it is raining in Seattle right now**. Taken together, Statements (1) and (2) are Sufficient.

> A̶D̶
> B(C)E

The correct answer is **(C)**.

Know Your Relationships

There are a number of shapes that pop up again and again in Geometry Data Sufficiency questions: squares, circles, 30–60–90 triangles, 45–45–90 triangles, and equilateral triangles in particular.

These shapes appear more frequently because a little information goes a long way.

For a square, if you know the value of any one of the following elements, you can calculate the rest: side length, diagonal length, perimeter, area.

For a circle, if you know the value of any one of the following elements, you can calculate the rest: radius, diameter, circumference, and area.

For 30–60–90, 45–45–90 triangles, and equilateral triangles, if you know the value of any one of the following elements, you can calculate the rest: one side length and its corresponding angle, perimeter, area.

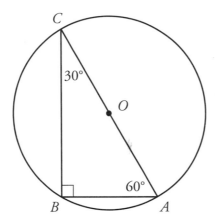

The center of the circle is O. Suppose you needed to find the length of segment BC. Decide whether each of the following values would be sufficient to answer the question:

    (1) The length of side AB
    (2) The length of OC
    (3) The circumference of the circle
    (4) The area of triangle ABC

If you said each statement by itself is sufficient, you're correct. Here's a brief explanation for each statement:

    (1) The ratio of side AB to side BC is $x : x\sqrt{3}$.
    (ex. if $AB = 3$, $BC = 3\sqrt{3}$)

(2) *OC* is a radius, which means that side *AC* is a diameter of the circle. The ratio of side *AC* to side *BC* is $2x : x\sqrt{3}$.
(ex. if $OC = 5$, $AC = 10$, and $BC = 5\sqrt{3}$)

(3) You can use the circumference to calculate the diameter, which is equal to side *AC*. The ratio of side *AC* to side *BC* is $2x : x\sqrt{3}$.
(ex. if the circumference $= 12\pi$, $AC = 12$, and $BC = 6\sqrt{3}$)

(4) The area of the triangle is equal to $\frac{1}{2}bh$. Sides *AB* and *BC* are the base and height, and the ratio of their lengths is $x : x\sqrt{3}$. Therefore, $A = \frac{1}{2}(x)(x\sqrt{3}) = \frac{1}{2}x^2\sqrt{3}$.

Statement (4) in particular has the potential to take up too much of your time, if you actually solve for *x*. You know the area will allow you to solve for *x*, and that you could use that value to solve for the length of *BC*. Since it's Data Sufficiency all that's important is that you can. By the way, even though the equation contains x^2, the triangle does cannot have negative side lengths, so you can ignore the negative solution.

When a circle, 30–60–90 triangle, or a 45–45–90 triangle appears in a Data Sufficiency question, remember how much other information you *can* know, without actually performing the computation.

Having one of these shapes is like having a nuclear weapon — you shouldn't actually use it, just know that you could!

Principles of Geometry

Suppose you are asked the following question:

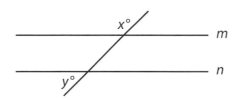

In the figure above, what is the value of $x + y$?

There are two important principles of Geometry. The first one is:

Don't assume what you don't know for sure.

In the picture above, lines *m* and *n* *look* parallel. But you have not been given any indication that they are. Without additional information, you are unable to answer the question.

Now suppose that you have been told that the lines are, in fact, parallel. You have now been given enough information to answer the question. When parallel lines are intersected by a third line, the eight angles created by the third line are all related.

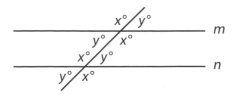

Now, even though you don't know the individual values of x and y, you know the sum $x + y$. A straight line has a degree measure of 180°, and the angles x and y together make up a straight line. Therefore, $x + y = 180$.

That brings us to the second principle:

Use every piece of information you do have to make further inferences.

6 General Geometry Approach

Let's use the following question to walk through the basic approach to geometry questions.

> Triangle *ABC* is inscribed in a Circle. If the length of side *AB* is 6, the length of side *AC* is 8, and *BC* is a diameter of the circle, what is the area of the circle?
>
> (A) 25   (B) 50   (C) 25π   (D) 50π   (E) 100π

Step 1: Draw or Redraw the Figure.

The question has described a triangle inscribed in a circle. On your scratch paper, you should draw this figure large enough for you to add in information (such as side lengths and angles). In general:

> If a question describes a figure: **Draw It**
> If a question shows a figure: **Redraw It**

For this question, you need a triangle drawn so that each side touches the circle. Since the question states that one side is a diameter, you should have one side go through the center of the circle, leaving you with something like this:

MANHATTAN
GMAT

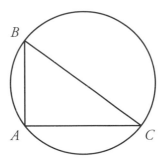

Now you're ready for the next step.

Step 2: Fill in the Given Information.

The question didn't just describe a figure; it also gave you some concrete information. You have made the figure large so that you can add any information the question gave you, such as side lengths.

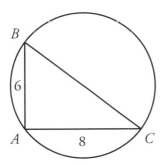

Now that the proper set-up work is complete, you can establish what you're looking for.

Step 3: Identify the Wanted Element.

Always know what value you are solving for. In this case, you need the area of the circle. The formula for area is $A = \pi r^2$.

In order to know the area, you need to know the radius of the circle. Now you're ready to begin solving.

Step 4: Infer from the Givens.

Now you have to use the given information to solve for the desired value. Most of the inferences you make in Geometry questions will give you the values of:

additional side lengths
additional angles

In this problem, there is an important inference you need to make. The question told you that side *BC* is a diameter of the circle. If one side of an inscribed triangle is a diameter of the circle, the triangle is a right triangle. You can infer that angle *BAC* is a right angle.

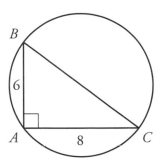

Now you're getting somewhere! Now that you know triangle *ABC* is a right triangle, you can use the Pythagorean Theorem to solve for the length of side *BC*. When possible, **create equations and solve for unknowns**.

$$6^2 + 8^2 = (BC)^2$$
$$36 + 64 = (BC)^2$$
$$100 = (BC)^2$$
$$10 = BC$$

Now you're ready for the final step.

Step 5: Find the Wanted Element.

If the diameter of the circle is 10, then the radius is 5. Finally, you can solve for the area:

$$A = \pi r^2$$
$$A = \pi(5)^2$$
$$A = 25\pi$$

Now you know the five basic steps to solve Geometry questions.

1) Draw or Redraw the Figure
2) Fill in the Given Information
3) Identify the Wanted Element
4) Infer from the Givens
5) Find the Wanted Element

MANHATTAN
GMAT

Shapes in Shapes

Many Geometry questions that contain figures will feature two or more shapes. If one shape is inside the other, you will probably need to find a bridge between the two shapes.

A bridge is a length that is common to both shapes.

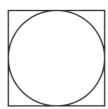

A circle is inscribed in a square with area 144.
What is the area of the circle?

To find the area of the circle, you will need the radius (because $A = \pi r^2$). The only information you've been provided, however, is about the square. You need a bridge.

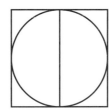

The line that you added to the figure is a diameter of the circle and is also the same length as the sides of the square. This is your bridge!

Find the length of the sides of the square to find the area of the circle.

If the area of the square is 144, then $s^2 = 144$. The square has sides of length 12.

That means the diameter of the circle is also 12. If the diameter is 12, then the radius is 6.

The rest is simple:

$$A = \pi r^2$$
$$A = \pi (6)^2$$
$$A = 36\pi$$

You found a bridge and correctly answered the question. Some other common bridges are shown below:

Triangle in Rectangle

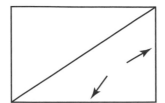

length + width of rectangle =
base + height of triangle

Triangle in Trapezoid

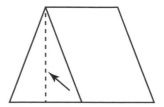

height of trapezoid =
height of triangle

Triangle in Circle

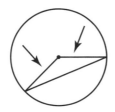

radii of circle =
sides of triangle

Square in Circle

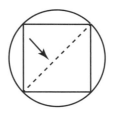

diameter of circle =
diagonal of square

Whenever problems involve shapes within shapes, look for a bridge.

Inscribed Triangles

There is one shape within a shape that deserves special mention. As we saw with the earlier example, **if one of the sides of an inscribed triangle is a *diameter* of the circle, then the triangle *must* be a *right triangle*.** Conversely, any right triangle inscribed in a circle must have the diameter of the circle as one of its sides.

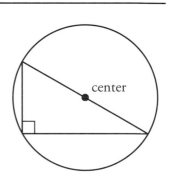

This rule is based on what we know about inscribed angles in a circle. Above right is a triangle that demonstrates the rule. The right angle (90°) lies opposite a semicircle, which is an arc that measures 180°.

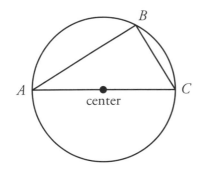

In the inscribed triangle to the left, triangle *ABC* must be a right triangle, since *AC* is a diameter of the circle.

Represent Angles with Variables

We'll use the following question to demonstrate a useful technique for questions that involve figures with unknown angles.

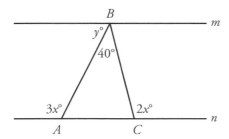

If lines *m* and *n* in the figure above are parallel, what is *y*?

Remember **Step 1:** when Geometry questions involve a figure, redraw it.

Step 2: Fill in the Given Information. The only extra information is that lines *m* and *n* are parallel.

Step 3: Identify the Wanted Element. You need the value of *y*. If you're not sure yet how you'll solve for *y*, that's fine. Maybe during the next step you'll get a better idea.

Step 4: Infer from the Givens. To answer this question, you need to fill in additional angles in your figure. Although you don't know any actual values (aside from 40°), you can **use the variables you already have**.

A straight line has 180 degrees. Therefore, the sum of two angles that form a straight line must also be 180. Angles *BAC* and *BCA* both have supplementary angles.

$$BAC + 3x = 180 \quad \longrightarrow \quad BAC = 180 - 3x$$
$$BCA + 2x = 180 \quad \longrightarrow \quad BCA = 180 - 2x$$

Add these values to the figure.

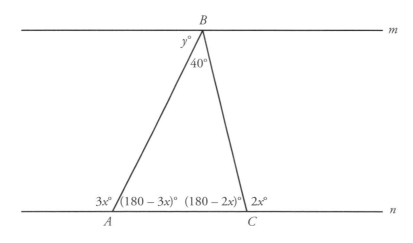

You still don't have concrete numbers, but you do have enough information to create an equation. You know the angles in triangle ABC must add up to 180.

$$(180 - 3x) + (180 - 2x) + 40 = 180$$
$$400 - 5x = 180$$
$$220 = 5x$$
$$44 = x$$

Now that you know the value of x, you can fill in all the angles.

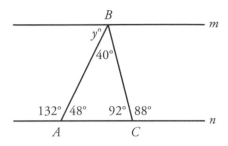

Now we have the information we need for the 5th and final step: Find the Wanted Element. Because m and n are parallel, we know that y must be equal to the degree measure of angle BAC. Therefore, $y = 48$.

Unspecified Amounts

Some Geometry problems on the GMAT will not specify any amounts. Just as with other GMAT problems with unspecified amounts, solve these problems by **picking numbers**.

> If the length of the side of a cube decreases by one-half, by what percentage will the volume of the cube decrease?

First, consider the formula involved here. The volume of a cube is defined by the formula $V = s^3$, where s represents the length of a side. Then, pick a number for the length of the side of the cube.

Say that the cube has a side of 2 units. Note that this is a "smart" number to pick because it is divisible by 2 (the denominator of one-half). Then, its volume $= s^3 = 2 \times 2 \times 2 = 8$.

If the cube's side decreases by one-half, its new length is $2 - \dfrac{1}{2}(2) = 1$ unit.

Its new volume $= s^3 = 1 \times 1 \times 1 = 1$.

Determine percent decrease as follows:

$$\frac{\text{change}}{\text{original}} = \frac{8-1}{8} = \frac{7}{8} = 0.875 = 87.5\% \text{ decrease}$$

Problem Set

1. If the length of an edge of Cube A is one-third the length of an edge of Cube B, what is the ratio of the volume of Cube A to the volume of Cube B?

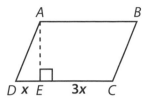

2. *ABCD* is a parallelogram (see figure above). The ratio of *DE* to *EC* is 1 : 3. *AE* has a length of 3. If quadrilateral *ABCE* has an area of 21, what is the area of *ABCD*?

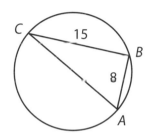

3. Triangle *ABC* is inscribed in a circle, such that *AC* is a diameter of the circle (see figure above). If *AB* has a length of 8 and *BC* has a length of 15, what is the circumference of the circle?

4. Triangle *ABC* is inscribed in a circle, such that *AC* is a diameter of the circle and angle *BAC* is 45°. If the area of triangle *ABC* is 72 square units, how much larger is the area of the circle than the area of triangle *ABC*?

5.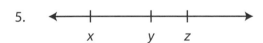

    On the number line above, is $xy < 0$?

    (1) Zero is to the left of *y* on the number line above.

    (2) *xy* and *yz* have opposite signs.

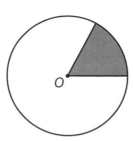

6.   If O represents the center of a circular clock and the point of the clock hand is on the circumference of the circle, does the shaded sector of the clock represent more than 10 minutes?

   (1)   The clock hand has a length of 10.

   (2)   The area of the sector is more than 16π.

P

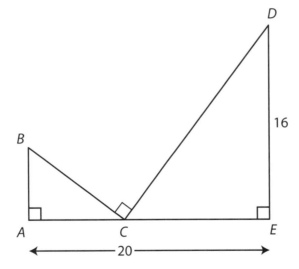

7.   What is the area of triangle ABC?

   (1)   Side $DC = 20$

   (2)   Side $AC = 8$

8.   The side of an equilateral triangle has the same length as the diagonal of a square. What is the area of the square?

   (1)   The height of the equilateral triangle is equal to $6\sqrt{3}$.

   (2)   The area of the equilateral triangle is equal to $36\sqrt{3}$.

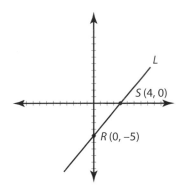

9.   Line *L* passes through points *R* (0, −5) and *S* (4, 0)(see figure above). Point *P* with
      coordinates (*x*, *y*) is a point on Line *L*. Is *xy* > 0?

      (1)   *x* > 4

      (2)   *y* > −5

Solutions

1. **1 to 27:** There are no specified amounts in this question, so you should pick numbers. You can say that Cube A has sides of length 1, and Cube B has sides of length 3.

> The volume of Cube A = $1 \times 1 \times 1 = 1$.
> The volume of Cube B = $3 \times 3 \times 3 = 27$.

Therefore, the ratio of the volume of Cube A to the volume of Cube B is $\dfrac{1}{27}$, or 1 to 27.

2. **24:** First, break quadrilateral *ABCE* into 2 pieces: a 3 by 3*x* rectangle and a right triangle with a base of *x* and a height of 3. Therefore, the area of quadrilateral *ABCE* is given by the following equation:

$$(3 \times 3x) + \frac{3 \times x}{2} = 9x + 1.5x = 10.5x$$

If *ABCE* has an area of 21, then $21 = 10.5x$, and $x = 2$. Quadrilateral *ABCD* is a parallelogram; thus, its area is equal to (base) × (height), or $4x \times 3$. Substitute the known value of 2 for *x* and simplify:

$$A = 4(2) \times 3 = 24$$

3. **17π:** If *AC* is a diameter of the circle, then inscribed triangle *ABC* is a right triangle, with *AC* as the hypotenuse. Therefore, you can apply the Pythagorean Theorem to find the length of *AC*:

$$8^2 + 15^2 = c^2$$
$$64 + 225 = c^2$$
$$289 = c^2$$
$$c = 17$$

You might also have recognized the common 8–15–17 right triangle.

The circumference of the circle is πd, or 17π.

4. **72π − 72:** If *AC* is a diameter of the circle, then angle *ABC* is a right angle. Therefore, triangle *ABC* is a 45–45–90 triangle, and the base and the height are equal. Assign the variable *x* to represent both the base and height:

$$A = \frac{bh}{2}$$
$$72 = \frac{(x)(x)}{2}$$
$$144 = x^2$$
$$12 = x$$

P

The base and the height of the triangle are equal to 12, and so the area of the triangle is $\frac{12 \times 12}{2} = 72$.

Because you have a 45–45–90 triangle, and the two legs are equal to 12, the common ratio tells you that the hypotenuse, which is also the diameter of the circle, is $12\sqrt{2}$. Therefore, the radius is equal to $6\sqrt{2}$ and the area of the circle, πr^2, equals 72π. The area of the circle is $72\pi - 72$ square units larger than the area of triangle *ABC*.

5. **C:** First note that this is a Yes/No Data Sufficiency question.

For *xy* to be negative, *x* and *y* need to have opposite signs. On the number line shown, this would only happen if zero falls between *x* and *y*. If zero is to the left of *x* on the number line shown, both *x* and *y* would be positive, so $xy > 0$. If zero is to the right of *y* on the number line shown, both *x* and *y* would be negative, so $xy > 0$.

(1) INSUFFICIENT: If zero is to the left of *y* on the number line above, zero could be between *x* and *y*. $xy < 0$ and the answer to the question is "yes." However, if 0 is to the left of *x*, $xy > 0$ and the answer is "no."

(2) INSUFFICIENT: *xy* and *yz* having opposite signs implies that one of the three variables has a different sign than the other two. If *x*, *y*, and *z* all have the same sign, *xy* and *yz* would have the same sign. Thus, this statement implies that zero does not fall to the left of *x* (which would make all three variables, as well as *xy* and *yz*, positive) nor to the right of *z* (which would make all three variables negative, and both *xy* and *yz* positive). The only two cases this statement allows are:

Zero is between *x* and *y*: *yz* is positive and *xy* is negative (the answer is "yes").
Zero is between *y* and *z*: *yz* is negative and *xy* is positive (the answer is "no").

(1) AND (2) SUFFICIENT: Statement (1) restricts zero to left of *y* on the number line. This rules out one of the two cases allowed by Statement (2), leaving only the case in which zero is between *x* and *y*. Thus, *xy* is negative, and the answer is a definite "yes."

The correct answer is C.

6. **E:** First of all, note that this is a Yes/No Data Sufficiency question.

The question "Does the shaded sector of the clock represent more than 10 minutes?" is really asking you about the area of a sector of a circle.

Since 10 minutes is 1/6 of an hour, you are being asked if the shaded region is equal to more than 1/6 of the area of the circle.

(1) INSUFFICIENT: The "clock hand" is equal to the radius. Knowing that the radius = 10 is enough to tell you that the entire area of the circle is equal to 100π. You can rephrase the question as, "Is the area of the shaded region more than one-sixth of 100π?" You can simplify 1/6 of 100π as such:

$$\frac{100\pi}{6} = \frac{50\pi}{3} = 16.\overline{6}\pi$$

Thus, the question can be rephrased as, "Is the area of the shaded region more than $16.\overline{6}\pi$?" However, you don't know anything about the area of the shaded region from this statement alone.

(2) INSUFFICIENT: The area of the sector is more than 16π. By itself, this does not tell you anything about whether the area of the sector is more than 1/6 the area of the circle, since you do not know the area of the entire circle.

(1) AND (2) INSUFFICIENT: The area of the entire circle is 100π, and the area of the sector is "more than 16π."

Since 1/6 of the area of the circle is actually $16.\overline{6}\pi$, knowing that the area of the sector is "more than 16π" is still insufficient—the area of the sector could be 16.1π or something much larger.

The correct answer is E.

7. **D:** First, note that this is a Value Data Sufficiency question.

A big mistake in this problem would be to plunge into the statements without fully analyzing and exploiting the diagram. You've got two right triangles that share a 90-degree span on either side of point C. What's going on here?

As it turns out, *these triangles are similar.*

Any time two triangles *each* have a right angle and *also* share an additional right angle (or, in this case, the 90 degree span on either side of point C), they will be similar. But if you didn't know that, you could easily uncover that fact by labeling any angle as x and labeling the others in terms of x:

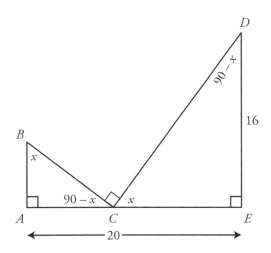

Once you determine that both triangles have the angles 90, x, and $90 - x$, you may wish to redraw one or both of them in order to get them facing in the same direction.

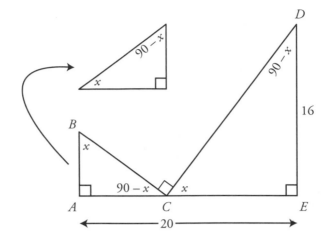

Now, let's decide exactly what the question is asking. You need the area of triangle *ABC*. In order to get that, you need the base and height of that triangle.

Since the two triangles are right triangles, if you had any two sides of triangle *ABC*, you could get the third. Because the two triangles are similar, you could use any two sides of triangle *EDC* (note that you already have that side *DE* = 16), as well as the ratio of one triangle's size to the other, to get the third side of *EDC* as well as all three sides of *ABC*.

Thus, the rephrased question is, "What are any two sides of *ABC*, or what is any additional side of *EDC* plus the ratio of the size of each triangle to the other?"

(1) SUFFICIENT: Side *DC* = 20. Use the 20 and the 16 to get, via the Pythagorean Theorem, that side *CE* = 12 (or simply recognize that you have a multiple of a 3–4–5 triangle). If *CE* = 12 then *AC* = 8. Thus, you have all three sides of *EDC*, plus the ratio of one triangle to the other (side *AC*, which equals 8, matches up with side *DE*, which equals 16; thus the smaller triangle is one-half the side of the larger).

Note that it is totally unnecessary to calculate further (once you have correctly rephrased the question, don't waste time doing more than is needed to answer the rephrase!), but if you are curious:

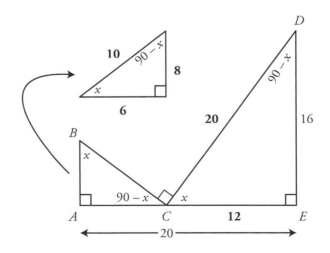

(2) SUFFICIENT: Side $AC = 8$. Note that this gives you the same information as Statement 1. If $AC = 8$, then $CE = 12$ and you can calculate all three sides of EDC. Once you know that side $AC = 8$ and that AC matches up with DE, which is equal to 16, you can know all three sides of ABC, as above.

The correct answer is D.

8. **D:** No calculation is needed to solve this problem. Both equilateral triangles and squares are *regular figures*—those that can change size, but never shape.

Regular figures (squares, equilaterals, circles, spheres, cubes, 45–45–90 triangles, 30–60–90 triangles, and others) are those for which you only need one measurement to know *every* measurement. For instance, if you have the radius of a circle, you can get the diameter, circumference, and area. If you have a 45–45–90 or 30–60–90 triangle, you only need *one* side to get all three. In this problem, if you have the side of an equilateral, you could get the height, area, and perimeter. If you have the side of a square, you could get the diagonal, area, and perimeter.

If you have *two* regular figures, as you do in this problem, and you know how they are related numerically ("the side of an equilateral triangle has the same length as the diagonal of a square"), then you can safely conclude that *any* measurement for *either* figure will give you *any* measurement for either figure.

The question can be rephrased as, *"What is the length of any part of either figure?"*

1) This gives you the height of the triangle. SUFFICIENT.
2) This gives you the area of the triangle. SUFFICIENT.

If you really wanted to "prove" that the answer is D, you could waste a lot of time:

From statement 1, if the height of the equilateral is $6\sqrt{3}$, then the side = 12, because heights and sides of equilaterals always exist in that ratio (the height is always one-half the side times $\sqrt{3}$). Then you would know that the diagonal of the square was also equal to 12, and from there you could use the 45–45–90 formula to conclude that the side of the square was $\dfrac{12}{\sqrt{2}}$, and therefore that the area was $\dfrac{144}{2}$, or 72.

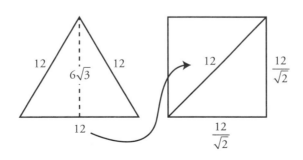

Similarly, from statement 2, you could conclude that if the area of the triangle is $36\sqrt{3}$, then the base times the height is $72\sqrt{3}$, and that since the side and height of an equilateral always exist in a fixed ratio (as above, the height is always one-half the side times $\sqrt{3}$), that the side is 12 and the height is $6\sqrt{3}$. Then, as above, you would know that the diagonal of the square was also equal to 12, and from there you could use the 45–45–90 formula to conclude that the side of the square was $\dfrac{12}{\sqrt{2}}$, and therefore that the area was $\dfrac{144}{2}$, or 72.

Who's got the time? This is a logic problem more than it is a math problem. If you understand the logic behind *regular figures*, you can answer this question in under 30 seconds with no math whatsoever.

The correct answer is D.

9. **A:** First, note that this is a Yes/No Data Sufficiency question.

Line *L* passes through three quadrants:

Quadrant I, where x and y are both positive, so $xy > 0$ and the answer is "yes."
Quadrant III, where x and y are both negative, so $xy > 0$ and the answer is "yes."
Quadrant IV, where x is positive and y is negative, so $xy < 0$ and the answer is "no."

If you can determine what quadrant point *P* is in, you will have sufficient information to answer the question. Also, if you know that point *P* is in either quadrant I or quadrant III, that would also be sufficient.

(1) SUFFICIENT: If $x > 4$, then Point *P* is in Quadrant I, so $xy > 0$ and the answer is "yes."

(2) INSUFFICIENT: If $y > -5$, then Point *P* could be in either Quadrant I ($xy > 0$) or Quadrant IV ($xy < 0$).

The correct answer is A.

Chapter 7 of Geometry

Extra Geometry

In This Chapter...

Chapter 7:

Extra Geometry

Typically, difficult geometry problems draw on the *same* geometric principles as easier problems. The GMAT usually makes problems more difficult by adding steps. For instance, to solve Problem Solving #145 in *The Official Guide for GMAT Quantitative Review, 2nd Edition*, you have to complete several steps, using both Triangle concepts and Circle concepts. However, once you have labeled the diagram appropriately, each step is itself straightforward. Likewise, Problem Solving #228 in *The Official Guide for GMAT Review, 13th Edition* does not contain fundamentally difficult coordinate-plane geometry. What makes #228 hard is its hybrid nature: it is a Combinatorics problem in a Coordinate-Plane disguise.

All that said, a few miscellaneous topics in geometry may be called advanced. These topics rarely appear on easier problems.

Maximum Area of Polygons

In some problems, the GMAT may require you to determine the maximum or minimum area of a given figure. This condition could be stated *explicitly*, as in Problem Solving questions ("What is the maximum area of...?"), or *implicitly*, as in Data Sufficiency questions ("Is the area of rectangle *ABCD* less than 30?"). Following are two shortcuts that can help you optimize certain problems quickly.

Maximum Area of a Quadrilateral

Perhaps the best-known maximum area problem is to maximize the area of a quadrilateral (usually a rectangle) with a *fixed perimeter*. If a quadrilateral has a fixed perimeter, say, 36 inches, it can take a variety of shapes:

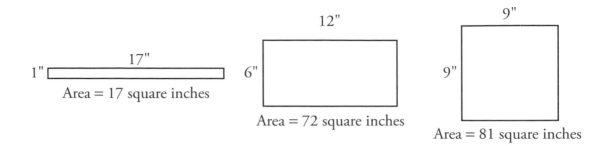

Of these figures, the one with the largest area is the square. This is a general rule: **Of all quadrilaterals with a given perimeter, the *square* has the largest area.** This is true even in cases involving non-integer lengths. For instance, of all quadrilaterals with a perimeter of 25 feet, the one with the largest area is a square with 25/4 = 6.25 feet per side.

This principle can also be turned around to yield the following corollary: **Of all quadrilaterals with a given area, the *square* has the minimum perimeter.**

Both of these principles can be generalized for *n* sides: a regular polygon with all sides equal (and pushed outward if necessary) will maximize area for a given perimeter and minimize perimeter for a given area.

Maximum Area of a Parallelogram or Triangle

Another common optimization problem involves maximizing the area of a *triangle or parallelogram with given side lengths*.

For instance, there are many triangles with two sides 3 and 4 units long. Imagine that the two sides of length 3 and 4 are on a hinge. The third side can have various lengths:

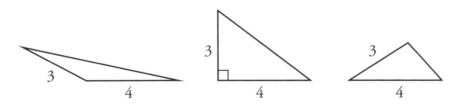

There are many corresponding parallelograms with two sides 3 and 4 units long:

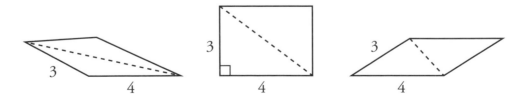

The area of a triangle is given by $A = \frac{1}{2}bh$ and the area of a parallelogram is given by $A = bh$. Because both of these formulas involve the perpendicular height h, the maximum area of each figure is achieved when the 3-unit side is perpendicular to the 4-unit side, so that the height is 3 units. All the other figures have lesser heights. (Note that in this case, the triangle of maximum area is the famous 3–4–5 right triangle.) If the sides are not perpendicular, then the figure is squished, so to speak.

The general rule is this: **if you are given two sides of a triangle or parallelogram, you can maximize the area by placing those two sides *perpendicular* to each other.**

Since the rhombus is simply a special case of a parallelogram, this rule holds for rhombuses as well. All sides of a rhombus are equal. Thus, you can maximize the area of a rhombus with a given side length by making the rhombus into a square.

Function Graphs and Quadratics

You can think of the slope-intercept form of a linear equation as a function: $y = f(x) = mx + b$. That is, you input the x-coordinate into the function $f(x) = mx + b$, and the output is the y-coordinate of the point that you plot on the line.

You can apply this process more generally. For instance, imagine that $y = f(x) = x^2$. Then you can generate the graph for $f(x)$ by plugging in a variety of values for x and getting values for y. The points (x, y) that you find lie on the graph of $y = f(x) = x^2$.

x	$f(x) = y$	Point
-3	$(-3)^2 = 9$	$(-3, 9)$
-2	$(-2)^2 = 4$	$(-2, 4)$
-1	$(-1)^2 = 1$	$(-1, 1)$
0	$0^2 = 0$	$(0, 0)$
1	$1^2 = 1$	$(1, 1)$
2	$2^2 = 2$	$(2, 4)$
3	$3^2 = 9$	$(3, 9)$

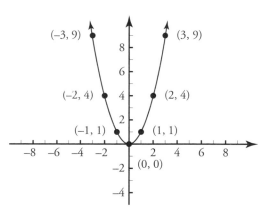

This curved graph is called a **parabola**. Any function of the form $f(x) = ax^2 + bx + c$, where a, b, and c are constants, is called a **quadratic function** and can be plotted as a parabola in the coordinate plane. Depending on the value of a, the curve will have different shapes:

Positive value for a   Curve opens upward
Negative value for a   Curve opens downward

Large |a| (absolute value)   Narrow curve
Small |a| Wide curve

The parabola will always open upward or downward.

The most important questions you will be asked about the parabola are these:

(1) How many times does the parabola touch the *x*-axis?
(2) If the parabola does touch the *x*-axis, where does it touch?

In other words, how many *x*-intercepts are there, and what are they?

The reason these questions are important is that the *x*-axis is the line representing $y = 0$. In other words, the parabola touches the *x*-axis at those values of *x* that make $f(x) = 0$. Therefore, these values solve the quadratic equation given by $f(x) = ax^2 + bx + c = 0$.

You can solve for zero by factoring and solving the equation directly. Alternatively, you might plug in points and draw the parabola. Finally, for some very difficult problems, you can use the quadratic formula:

$$x = \frac{-b \pm \sqrt{b^2 - 4ac}}{2a}$$

One solution is $\dfrac{-b + \sqrt{b^2 - 4ac}}{2a}$, and the other is $\dfrac{-b - \sqrt{b^2 - 4ac}}{2a}$.

The vast majority of GMAT quadratic problems can be solved *without* using the quadratic formula. If you do apply this formula, the advantage is that you can quickly tell how many solutions the equation has by looking at just one part: the expression under the radical sign, $b^2 = 4ac$. This expression is known as the **discriminant**, because it discriminates or distinguishes three cases for the number of solutions to the equation, as follows:

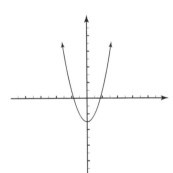

(1) If $b^2 - 4ac > 0$, then the square root operation yields a positive number. The quadratic formula produces *two roots* of the quadratic equation. This means that the parabola crosses the *x*-axis twice and has two *x*-intercepts.

(2) If $b^2 - 4ac = 0$, then the square root operation yields zero. The quadratic formula only produces *one root* of the quadratic equation. This means that the parabola just touches the *x*-axis once and has just one *x*-intercept.

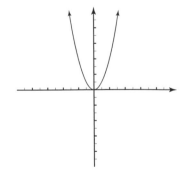

(3) If $b^2 - 4ac < 0$ then the square root operation cannot be performed. This means that the quadratic formula produces *no roots* of the quadratic equation, and the parabola never touches the x-axis (it has no x-intercepts).

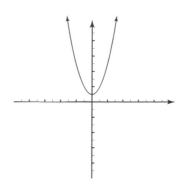

It is possible for the GMAT to ask you to graph other non-linear functions of x. The following points lie at the heart of all problems involving graphs of other non-linear functions, as well as lines and parabolas.

(1) If a point lies on the graph, then you can plug its coordinates into the equation $y = f(x)$. Conversely, if a value of x and a value of y satisfy the equation $y = f(x)$, then the point (x, y) lies on the graph of $f(x)$.

(2) To find x-intercepts, find the values of x for which $y = f(x) = 0$.

(3) To find y-intercepts, set $x = 0$ and find $y = f(0)$.

Perpendicular Bisectors

The perpendicular bisector of a line segment forms a 90° angle with the segment and divides the segment exactly in half. Questions about perpendicular bisectors are rare on the GMAT, but they do appear occasionally.

7

> If the coordinates of point *A* are (2, 2) and the coordinates of point *B* are (0, −2), what is the equation of the perpendicular bisector of line segment *AB*?

The key to solving perpendicular bisector problems is remembering this property: the perpendicular bisector has the **negative reciprocal slope** of the line segment it bisects. That is, the product of the two slopes is −1. (The only exception occurs when one line is horizontal and the other line is vertical, since vertical lines have undefined slopes).

(1) Find the slope of segment *AB*.

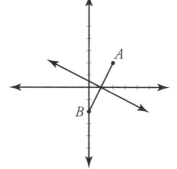

$$\text{slope} = \frac{\text{rise}}{\text{run}} = \frac{y_1 - y_2}{x_1 + x_2} = \frac{2 - (-2)}{2 - 0} = \frac{4}{2} = 2$$

The slope of *AB* is 2.

(2) Find the slope of the perpendicular bisector of *AB*.

Since perpendicular lines have negative reciprocal slopes, flip the fraction and change the sign to find the slope of the perpendicular bisector.

Again, the slope of *AB* is 2, or $\frac{2}{1}$.

Therefore, the slope of the perpendicular bisector of AB is $-\dfrac{1}{2}$.

Now you know that the equation of the perpendicular bisector has the following form:

$$y = -\dfrac{1}{2}x + b$$

However, you still need to find the value of b (the y-intercept). To do this, you will need to find one point on the perpendicular bisector. Then you will plug the coordinates of this point into the equation above.

(3) Find the midpoint of AB.

The perpendicular bisector passes through the midpoint of AB. Thus, if you find the midpoint of AB, you will have found a point on the perpendicular bisector. Organize a chart such as the one shown below to find the coordinates of the midpoint. Simply write the x- and y-coordinates of A and B. The coordinates of the midpoint will be the numbers right in between each pair of x- and y-coordinates. In other words, the x-coordinate of the midpoint is the *average* of the x-coordinates of A and B. Likewise, the y-coordinate of the midpoint is the *average* of the y-coordinates of A and B. This process will yield the midpoint of any line segment.

	x	y
A	2	2
Midpoint	**1**	**0**
B	0	−2

(4) Put the information together.

To find the value of b (the y-intercept), substitute the coordinates of the midpoint for x and y.

$$0 = -\dfrac{1}{2}(1) + b$$

$$b = \dfrac{1}{2}$$

The perpendicular bisector of segment AB has the equation: $y = -\dfrac{1}{2}x + \dfrac{1}{2}$.

In summary, the following rules can be given:

- **Parallel lines have equal slopes.** $m_1 = m_2$.

- **Perpendicular lines have negative reciprocal slopes.** $\dfrac{-1}{m_1} = m_2$, or $m_1 \cdot m_2 = -1$.

• The midpoint between point $A(x_1, y_1)$ and point $B(x_2, y_2)$ is $\left(\dfrac{x_1 + x_2}{2}, \dfrac{y_1 + y_2}{2} \right)$

The Intersection of Two Lines

Recall that a line in the coordinate plane is defined by a linear equation relating x and y. That is, if a point (x, y) lies on the line, then those values of x and y satisfy the equation. For instance, the point $(3, 2)$ lies on the line defined by the equation $y = 4x - 10$, since the equation is true when you plug in $x = 3$ and $y = 2$:

$y = 4x - 10$
$2 = 4(3) - 10 = 12 - 10$
$2 = 2$ TRUE

On the other hand, the point $(7, 5)$ does not lie on that line, because the equation is false when you plug in $x = 7$ and $y = 5$:

$y = 4x - 10$
$5 = 4(7) - 10 = 28 - 10 = 18?$ FALSE

So, what does it mean when two lines intersect in the coordinate plane? It means that at the point of intersection, *both* equations representing the lines are true. That is, the pair of numbers (x, y) that represents the point of intersection solves *both* equations. Finding this point of intersection is equivalent to solving a system of two linear equations. You can find the intersection by using algebra more easily than by graphing the two lines.

7

> At what point does the line represented by $y = 4x - 10$ intersect the line represented by $2x + 3y = 26$?

Since $y = 4x - 10$, replace y in the second equation with $4x - 10$ and solve for x:

$2x + 3(4x - 10) = 26$
$2x + 12x - 30 = 26$
$14x = 56$
$x = 4$

Now solve for y. You can use either equation, but the first one is more convenient:

$y = 4x - 10$
$y = 4(4) - 10$
$y = 16 - 10 = 6$

Thus, the point of intersection of the two lines is $(4, 6)$.

If two lines in a plane do not intersect, then the lines are parallel. If this is the case, there is *no* pair of numbers (x, y) that satisfies both equations at the same time.

Two linear equations can represent two lines that intersect at a single point, or they can represent parallel lines that never intersect. There is one other possibility: the two equations might represent the same line. In this case, infinitely many points (x, y) along the line satisfy the two equations (which must actually be the same equation in two disguises).

7

Problem Set

1. What is the maximum possible area of a quadrilateral with a perimeter of 80 centimeters?

2. What is the minimum possible perimeter of a quadrilateral with an area of 1,600 square feet?

3. What is the maximum possible area of a parallelogram with one side of length 2 meters and a perimeter of 24 meters?

4. What is the maximum possible area of a triangle with a side of length 7 units and another side of length 8 units?

5. The lengths of the two shorter legs of a right triangle add up to 40 units. What is the maximum possible area of the triangle?

6. What is x in the diagram below?

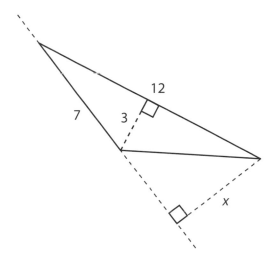

P

7. The line represented by the equation $y = -2x + 6$ is the perpendicular bisector of the line segment AB. If A has the coordinates $(7, 2)$, what are the coordinates for B?

8. How many x-intercepts does $f(x) = x^2 + 3x + 3$ have?

9. The line represented by the equation $y = x$ is the perpendicular bisector of line segment AB. If A has the coordinates $(-3, 3)$, what are the coordinates of B?

10. What are the coordinates for the point on Line AB (see figure at right) that is three times as far from A as from B, and that is in between points A and B?

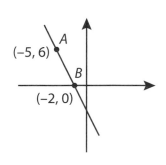

Solutions

1. **400 cm²:** The quadrilateral with maximum area for a given perimeter is a square, which has four equal sides. Therefore, the square that has a perimeter of 80 centimeters has sides of length 20 centimeters each. Since the area of a square is the side length squared, the area = (20 cm)(20 cm) = 400 cm².

2. **160 ft:** The quadrilateral with minimum perimeter for a given area is a square. Since the area of a square is the side length squared, you can solve the equation $x^2 = 1{,}600$ ft² for the side length x, yielding $x = 40$ ft. The perimeter, which is four times the side length, is (4)(40 ft) = 160 ft.

3. **20 m²:** If one side of the parallelogram is 2 meters long, then the opposite side must also be 2 meters long. You can solve for the unknown sides, which are equal in length, by writing an equation for the perimeter: $24 = 2(2) + 2x$, with x as the unknown side. Solving, you get $x = 10$ meters. The parallelogram with these dimensions and maximum area is a *rectangle* with 2-meter and 10-meter sides. Thus the maximum possible area of the figure is (2 m)(10 m) = 20 m².

4. **28 square units:** A triangle with two given sides has maximum area if these two sides are placed at right angles to each other. For this triangle, one of the given sides can be considered the base, and the other side can be considered the height (because they meet at a right angle). Thus you plug these sides into the formula $A = \dfrac{1}{2}bh$: $A = \dfrac{1}{2}(7)(8) = 28$.

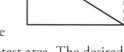

5. **200 square units:** You can think of a right triangle as half of a rectangle. Constructing this right triangle with legs adding to 40 is equivalent to constructing the rectangle with a perimeter of 80. Since the area of the triangle is half that of the rectangle, you can use the previously mentioned technique for maximizing the area of a rectangle: of all rectangles with a given perimeter, the *square* has the greatest area. The desired rectangle is thus a 20 by 20 square, and the right triangle has area (1/2)(20)(20) = 200 units.

6. **36/7:** You can calculate the area of the triangle, using the side of length 12 as the base:

$$(1/2)(12)(3) = 18$$

Next, use the side of length 7 as the base and write the equation for the area:

$$(1/2)(7)(x) = 18$$

Now solve for x, the unknown height:

$$7x = 36$$
$$x = 36/7$$

Alternately, the large overall triangle is similar to the small triangle on the left side of the picture because they have the same angle measurements (both are right triangles, and they also share one angle in the far left tip of the diagram). Draw these two triangles side by side and match up the sides. The hypotenuse of 7 in the smaller triangle "matches up" with the hypotenuse of 12 in the larger triangle, so the ratio of the two triangles is 12/7. Multiply the known leg 3 in the smaller triangle by the ratio multiplier 12/7 to get $3 \times 12/7 = 36/7$. The value of x is 36/7.

7. **(–1, –2)**: If $y = -2x + 6$ is the perpendicular bisector of segment AB, then the line containing segment AB must have a slope of 0.5 (the negative inverse of –2). You can represent this line with the equation $y = 0.5x + b$. Substitute the coordinates (7, 2) into the equation to find the value of b.

	x	y
A	7	2
Midpoint	3	0
B	–1	–2

$$2 = 0.5(7) + b.$$
$$b = -1.5$$

The line containing AB is $y = 0.5x - 1.5$.

Find the point at which the perpendicular bisector intersects AB by setting the two equations, $y = -2x + 6$ and $y = 0.5x - 1.5$, equal to each other.

$$-2x + 6 = 0.5x - 1.5$$
$$2.5x = 7.5$$
$$x = 3; y = 0$$

The two lines intersect at (3, 0), which is the midpoint of AB.

Use a chart to find the coordinates of B.

8. **None**: There are three ways to solve this equation. The first is to attempt to factor the quadratic equation to find solutions. Since no two integers multiply to 3 and add to 3, this strategy fails.

The second approach is to pick numbers for x, solve for $f(x)$ (plotted as y in the coordinate plane), and plot these (x, y) pairs to determine the shape of the parabola. An example of this technique is displayed to the right.

x	$x^2 + 3x + 3 = y$	Point
–3	$9 - 9 + 3 = 3$	(–3, 3)
–2	$4 - 6 + 3 = 1$	(–2, 1)
–1	$1 - 3 + 3 = 1$	(–1, 1)
0	$0 + 0 + 3 = 3$	(0, 3)
1	$1 + 3 + 3 = 7$	(1, 7)

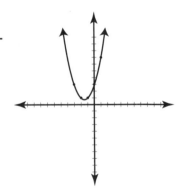

This approach demonstrates that the parabola never touches the x-axis. There are no x-intercepts.

The third method is to use the discriminant of the quadratic equation to count the number of x-intercepts.

First, identify the coefficients of each term. The function is $f(x) = x^2 + 3x + 3$. Matching this up to the definition of the standard quadratic equation, $f(x) = ax^2 + bx + c$, you have $a = 1$, $b = 3$, and $c = 3$.

Next, write the discriminant from the quadratic formula (the expression that is under the radical sign in the quadratic formula):

$$b^2 - 4ac = 3^2 - 4(1)(3)$$
$$= 9 - 12$$
$$= -3$$

Since the discriminant is less than zero, you cannot take its square root. This means that there is no solution to the equation $f(x) = x^2 + 3x + 3 = 0$, so the function's graph does not touch the x-axis. There are no x-intercepts.

9. **(3, –3):** Perpendicular lines have negative inverse slopes. Therefore, if $y = x$ is perpendicular to segment AB, you know that the slope of the perpendicular bisector is 1, and therefore the slope of segment AB is –1. The line containing segment AB takes the form of $y = -x + b$. To find the value of b, substitute the coordinates of A, $(-3, 3)$, into the equation:

$$3 = -(-3) + b$$
$$b = 0$$

The line containing segment AB is $y = -x$.

Find the point at which the perpendicular bisector intersects AB by setting the two equations, $y = x$ and $y = -x$, equal to each other:

$$x = -x$$
$$x = 0; y = 0$$

The two lines intersect at $(0, 0)$, which is the midpoint of AB. Use a chart to find the coordinates of B.

10. **(–2.75, 1.5):** The point in question is 3 times farther from A than it is from B. You can represent this fact by labeling the point $3x$ units from A and x units from B as shown, giving a total distance of $4x$ between the two points. If you drop vertical lines from the point and from A to the x-axis, you get 2 similar triangles, the smaller of which is a quarter of the larger. (You can get this relationship from the fact that the larger triangle's hypotenuse is 4 times larger than the hypotenuse of the smaller triangle.)

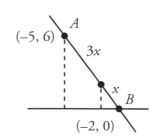

The horizontal distance between points A and B is 3 units (from –2 to –5). Therefore, $4x = 3$, and $x = 0.75$. The horizontal distance from B to the point is x, or 0.75 units. The x-coordinate of the point is 0.75 away from –2, or –2.75.

The vertical distance between points A and B is 6 units (from 0 to 6).

Therefore, $4x = 6$, and $x = 1.5$. The vertical distance from B to the point is x, or 1.5 units. The y-coordinate of the point is 1.5 away from 0, or 1.5.

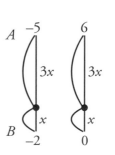

MANHATTAN
GMAT

Appendix A

of Geometry

Official Guide Problem Sets

In This Chapter...

Official Guide Problem Sets

Now that you have completed *Geometry*, it is time to test your skills on problems that have actually appeared on real GMAT exams over the past several years.

The problem sets that follow are composed of questions from two books published by the Graduate Management Admission Council® (the organization that develops the official GMAT exam):

> *The Official Guide for GMAT Review, 13th Edition*
> *The Official Guide for GMAT Quantitative Review, 2nd Edition*

These books contain quantitative questions that have appeared on past official GMAT exams. (The questions contained therein are the property of The Graduate Management Admission Council, which is not affiliated in any way with Manhattan GMAT.)

Although the questions in *The Official Guides* have been "retired" (they will not appear on future official GMAT exams), they are great practice questions.

In order to help you practice effectively, we have categorized every problem in *The Official Guides* by topic and subtopic. On the following pages, you will find two categorized lists:

1. **Problem Solving:**   Lists Problem Solving Geometry questions contained in *The Official Guides* and categorizes them by subtopic.

2. **Data Sufficiency:**   Lists Data Sufficiency Geometry questions contained in *The Official Guides* and categorizes them by subtopic.

Books 1 through 8 of Manhattan GMAT's Strategy Guide series each contain a unique *Official Guide* list that pertains to the specific topic of that particular book. If you complete all the practice problems contained on the *Official Guide* lists in each of these 8 Manhattan GMAT Strategy Guide books, you will have completed every single question published in *The Official Guides*.

Problem Solving Set

This set is from *The Official Guide for GMAT Review, 13th Edition* (pages 20–23 & 152–185), and *The Official Guide for GMAT Quantitative Review, 2nd Edition* (pages 62–86).

Solve each of the following problems in a notebook, making sure to demonstrate how you arrived at each answer by showing all of your work and computations. If you get stuck on a problem, look back at the Geometry strategies and content contained in this guide to assist you.

Note: Problem numbers preceded by "D" refer to questions in the Diagnostic Test chapter of *The Official Guide for GMAT Review, 13th Edition* (pages 20–23).

Polygons:

13th Edition: 3, 13, 18, 78, 104, 121, 147, 166
Quantitative Review: 15, 24, 135, 139, 175

Triangles & Diagonals:

13th Edition: 75, 92, 159, 161, 165, 197, 206, D19
Quantitative Review: 44, 71, 76, 150, 157

Circles & Cylinders:

13th Edition: 36, 69, 175, 213, D20, D22, D5
Quantitative Review: 33, 141, 145, 153, 162

Lines & Angles:

13th Edition: 62, 210, D10
Quantitative Review: 7, 30

Coordinate Plane:

13th Edition: 7, 28, 43, 61, 202, 211, 228
Quantitative Review: 21, 83, 85, 102, 123

Data Sufficiency Set

This set is from *The Official Guide for GMAT Review, 13th Edition* (pages 24–26 & 274–291), and *The Official Guide for GMAT Quantitative Review, 2nd Edition* (pages 152–163).

Solve each of the following problems in a notebook, making sure to demonstrate how you arrived at each answer by showing all of your work and computations. If you get stuck on a problem, look back at the Geometry strategies and content contained in this guide to assist you.

Practice **rephrasing** both the questions and the statements. The majority of data sufficiency problems can be rephrased; however, if you have difficulty rephrasing a problem, try testing numbers to solve it. It is especially important that you familiarize yourself with the directions for data sufficiency problems, and that you memorize the 5 fixed answer choices that accompany all data sufficiency problems.

Note: Problem numbers preceded by "D" refer to questions in the Diagnostic Test chapter of *The Official Guide for GMAT Review, 13th Edition* (pages 24–26).

Polygons:

> *13th Edition:* 4, 42, 130, 145, D48
> *Quantitative Review:* 4, 60, 88

Triangles & Diagonals:

> *13th Edition:* 19, 56, 73, 79, 113, 119, 128, 149, 152, D28
> *Quantitative Review:* 19, 43, 65, 91, 114, 123

Circles & Cylinders:

> *13th Edition:* 30, 35, 102, 117, 122, 165, D36
> *Quantitative Review:* 58, 59, 95, 99

Lines & Angles:

> *13th Edition:* 166
> *Quantitative Review:* 72

Coordinate Plane:

> *13th Edition:* 11, 74, 129, 155, D39
> *Quantitative Review:* 22

ALL TEST PREP IS NOT THE SAME

MANHATTAN
GMAT

MANHATTAN
GRE®

MANHATTAN
LSAT

Elite test preparation from 99th percentile instructors.
Find out how we're different.

www.manhattanprep.com

mbaMission